Greater Than a Tourist Book Series
Reviews from Readers

I think the series is wonderful and beneficial for tourists to get information before visiting the city.

-Seckin Zumbul, Izmir Turkey

I am a world traveler who has read many trip guides but this one really made a difference for me. I would call it a heartfelt creation of a local guide expert instead of just a guide.

-Susy, Isla Holbox, Mexico

New to the area like me, this is a must have!

-Joe, Bloomington, USA

This is a good series that gets down to it when looking for things to do at your destination without having to read a novel for just a few ideas.

-Rachel, Monterey, USA

Good information to have to plan my trip to this destination.

-Pennie Farrell, Mexico

Great ideas for a port day.

-Mary Martin USA

Aptly titled, you won't just be a tourist after reading this book. You'll be greater than a tourist!

-Alan Warner, Grand Rapids, USA

Even though I only have three days to spend in San Miguel in an upcoming visit, I will use the author's suggestions to guide some of my time there. An easy read - with chapters named to guide me in directions I want to go.

-Robert Catapano, USA

Great insights from a local perspective! Useful information and a very good value!

-Sarah, USA

This series provides an in-depth experience through the eyes of a local. Reading these series will help you to travel the city in with confidence and it'll make your journey a unique one.

-Andrew Teoh, Ipoh, Malaysia

GREATER THAN A TOURIST- MONTANA USA

50 Travel Tips from a Local

CZYK Publishing Since 2011.

Greater Than a Tourist

Lock Haven, PA
All rights reserved.

ISBN: 9781706401315

>TOURIST

50 TRAVEL TIPS FROM A LOCAL

BOOK DESCRIPTION

Are you excited about planning your next trip? Do you want to try something new? Would you like some guidance from a local? If you answered yes to any of these questions, then this Greater Than a Tourist book is for you. Greater Than a Tourist-Montana, USA, by Laurie White offers the inside scoop on Montana. Most travel books tell you how to travel like a tourist. Although there is nothing wrong with that, as part of the Greater Than a Tourist series, this book will give you travel tips from someone who has lived at your next travel destination.

In these pages, you will discover advice that will help you throughout your stay. This book will not tell you exact addresses or store hours but instead will give you excitement and knowledge from a local that you may not find in other smaller print travel books.

Travel like a local. Slow down, stay in one place, and get to know the people and culture. By the time you finish this book, you will be eager and prepared to travel to your next destination.

Inside this travel guide book you will find:

- Insider tips from a local.

- Packing and planning list.

- List of travel questions to ask yourself or others while traveling.

- A place to write your travel bucket list.

OUR STORY

Traveling is a passion of the Greater than a Tourist book series creator. Lisa studied abroad in college, and for their honeymoon Lisa and her husband toured Europe. During her travels to Malta, an older man tried to give her some advice based on his own experience living on the island since he was a young boy. She was not sure if she should talk to the stranger but was interested in his advice. When traveling to some places she was wary to talk to locals because she was afraid that they weren't being genuine. Through her travels, Lisa learned how much locals had to share with tourists. Lisa created the Greater Than a Tourist book series to help connect people with locals. A topic that locals are very passionate about sharing.

TABLE OF CONTENTS

EXPERIENCE THE BEST OF MONTANA

DEDICATION

This book is dedicated to my family. Of all the places I could have been raised, I am so thankful my family chose Montana. Thank you to my parents, grandparents and sisters for always loving me and encouraging me to follow my dreams. Thank you to my husband, Josh, for sticking by me through the all the highs and lows and always believing in me. Lastly, I dedicate this book to Hailey and Gracie, my little adventure partners. Seeing the world through your eyes has shown me how beautiful the world truly is.

ABOUT THE AUTHOR

Laurie White has deep Montana roots. Her family has lived on this land since before Montana was a state, making her a proud seventh generation Montanan. Laurie was raised in Drummond, Montana, where she grew up helping out at her family's restaurant. She always enjoyed the stories told by the local ranchers, tales from visiting travelers and good conversations over a hearty home-style meal.

Despite living in Montana her whole life, Laurie never runs out of new and exciting Montana adventures. She enjoys writing about and photographing all the places she explores and sharing them with family and friends. She loves introducing her daughters to the wild beauty that is Montana and she is happy to be sharing her great state with you.

HOW TO USE THIS BOOK

The *Greater Than a Tourist* book series was written by someone who has lived in an area for over three months. The goal of this book is to help travelers either dream or experience different locations by providing opinions from a local. The author has made suggestions based on their own experiences. Please check before traveling to the area in case the suggested places are unavailable.

Travel Advisories: As a first step in planning any trip abroad, check the Travel Advisories for your intended destination.
https://travel.state.gov/content/travel/en/traveladvisories/traveladvisories.html

FROM THE PUBLISHER

Traveling can be one of the most important parts of a person's life. The anticipation and memories that you have are some of the best. As a publisher of the Greater Than a Tourist, as well as the popular *50 Things to Know* book series, we strive to help you learn about new places, spark your imagination, and inspire you. Wherever you are and whatever you do I wish you safe, fun, and inspiring travel.

Lisa Rusczyk Ed. D.
CZYK Publishing

WELCOME TO
> TOURIST

I'm in love with Montana. For other states, I have admiration, respect, recognition, even some affection. But with Montana it is love. And it's difficult to analyze love when you're in it.

— John Steinbeck

The first time I came across this quote I was at the Iron Horse Bar and Grill in Missoula. I looked up and it was displayed proudly high across the wall. This quote resonated deeply with me and quickly became my favorite Montana quote. I have traveled to some incredible places and seen some great sites, but I always come home with a deeper love for my home state. It is hard to analyze that love because Montana is more than a state to me. It is engrained in who I am.

Growing up in Montana, I have become accustomed to friendly strangers genuinely asking how my day is, courteous drivers waving me out in front of them and a sense of everyone looking out for one another. It is one of my favorite things about living in Montana and I miss it every time I leave home. I think you will find it refreshing too. So go ahead and wave back to the strangers you pass on our backcountry roads, enjoy a good conversation with a local and if it's solitude you're searching for, we've got plenty of that too.

There are many great reasons visitors love coming to Montana. The *Treasure State* is the perfect place to seek peace and connect with the land's untouched beauty and spectacular wildlife. It is also an outdoor adventurist's dream come true. From whitewater rafting to excellent downhill skiing to horseback riding along scenic mountain trails, Montana has an adventure for everyone.

There are also many excellent opportunities across the state to step back in time and experience historic Montana. Out history is full of fascinating stories of Native Americans, miners, cowboys and vigilantes. You can tour a ghost town, learn about Native American culture or even dig for dinosaur fossils.

Montana offers unique outdoor fun, stunning scenery and some of the friendliest folks around. I am honored to have the privilege to share my home state with you, fellow traveler. I hope that my insight helps you to plan your trip and fully experience Montana's grandeur. With these traveling tips, I give you Montana from an insider's perspective.

Montana

United States

Helena
Montana
Climate

	High	Low
January	30	11
February	36	15
March	46	23
April	56	31
May	65	39
June	74	47
July	84	53
August	83	51
September	71	41
October	57	31
November	42	20
December	31	11

GreaterThanaTourist.com

Temperatures are in Fahrenheit degrees.
Source: NOAA

WHAT YOU SHOULD KNOW BEFORE VISITING MONTANA

1. WELCOME TO THE GREATEST STATE IN AMERICA

Montana is one of those American states that exert a magnetism and inspire a loyalty far out of proportion to any sober appraisal.

– Brad Tyer

Okay, claiming Montana is the greatest state might be a little bold. Of course there are many other great states, but ask any Montanan and we will tell you that we live in the best state. As Montanans, we take a lot of pride in our state. We love it here! What's not to love? There's wide-open spaces, gorgeous scenery, unlimited outdoor fun, friendly neighbors, freedom, peace, solitude…I could go on and on, but you get the point. Montana is truly the *Last Best Place.*

Montanans are a friendly and welcoming bunch. Sure we may give the out-of-staters (sorry Californians!) a little bit of a hard time, but it's all in good fun and we expect the same when we are in another state. We might give the impression that we aren't very accepting of newcomers with our *Montana is Full* and *No Vacancy* bumper stickers. This is because we love our state just how it is. We don't want it overcrowded, overdeveloped or changed in any way by an influx of people.

However, deep down we are glad you are here. We know that tourism is important to our economy, but mostly we are just happy to be showing off our incredible state and we really are a welcoming bunch. I think you will find our warm Montana hospitality is right up there with that of those southerners. So let me be the first to say, welcome to *Big Sky Country*! I know you will enjoy our beautiful state and we are glad to have you!

2. MONTANA IS BIG— KNOW YOUR REGIONS

*It seems to me Montana is a
great splash of grandeur. The scale
is huge but not overpowering. The
land is rich with grass and color,
and the mountains are the kind I
would create if mountains were
ever put on my agenda.*

– John Steinbeck

Montana is huge! Spanning 147,042 square miles, it is the fourth largest state in the United States. Montana is bigger than many countries! It can take a full day to drive across Montana. Additionally, Montana's terrain varies greatly from one side of the state to the other. So before you come it is important to make a plan and know what you want to see. To make it a little easier, Montana is often broken down into regions.

Montana is broadly divided into two regions: Eastern Montana and Western Montana. Basically, Western Montana is where the mountains are and

Eastern Montana is where the plains are. It is further divided into six tourism regions: Glacier Country, Gold West Country, Russell Country, Yellowstone Country, Missouri River Country and Custer Country. Each area is distinct and offers unique tourist destinations. I will give you a quick run down of each region, but first lets look at the distinctions between Western and Eastern Montana.

Western Montana

Montana gets its name from *montaanus*, the Latin word for mountainous. This name is truly fitting on the western third of the state where the majestic Northern Rocky Mountains provide gorgeous timber-covered mountain scenery and picturesque valleys. There are over 100 named mountain ranges in Montana.

The Continental divide passes through Montana in a jagged pattern from Glacier National Park in the north to Yellowstone National Park in the southwestern part of the state. Water east of the divide flows towards the Atlantic and water west of the divide flows to the Pacific. Triple Divide Peak, located in Glacier National Park, is quite unique. It is one of only two hydrological apexes in North America (there are only three known hydrological apexes in the world!). Water flows from this point to three different oceans: the Pacific, Atlantic and Arctic.

Eastern Montana

As you head towards Eastern Montana, the mountains fade into gently rolling plains. The sky seems to stretch on forever above the beautiful prairies and you really get a sense of why Montana is called *Big Sky Country*. The impressive prairies can stretch for miles upon miles, only interrupted by the occasional wetland. There are a few forested areas scattered across the high areas, such as Custer Gallatin National Forest. Eastern Montana is also home to spectacular badlands.

Now, lets look at the six unique regions in Montana:

3. GLACIER COUNTRY

As the name implies, Glacier Country in Northwestern Montana is home to the incredible Glacier National Park. This area is known for its rugged glacier-carved peaks, alpine lakes and meadows full of wildflowers. This is a great place to enjoy a scenic hike to a glacier, pick huckleberries or see a mountain goat or grizzly bear (hopefully from a safe distance!).

The beauty extends far beyond the actual park and includes the Bitterroot Valley and numerous scenic lakes such as Flathead Lake and Lake Koocanusa. The larger cities in this region are Whitefish, a charming ski resort town, Kalispell, named after the Salish Indian word meaning *flat land above the lake*, and Missoula, often called the *Garden City*. There are also many charming, artsy mountain towns to visit.

4. GOLD WEST COUNTRY

Gold West Country is located in the southwest corner of the state between Glacier National Park and Yellowstone National Park. This area is stunning with snow-capped mountains often lasting late into summer, beautiful valleys and sparkling rivers. Here you will find Helena, the state capital of Montana, as well as the mining city of Butte.

Southwest Montana is called Gold West Country because of its rich mining history. There are many exciting opportunities to tour old ghost towns and venture into fascinating underground mines (only enter mines designated as safe). This region is also the perfect spot for exciting outdoor activities and relaxing in the area's many natural hot springs.

5. RUSSELL COUNTRY

Central Montana, or Russell Country, encompasses the north-central part of the state and includes the cities of Great Falls and Havre. This region is named after Charlie Russell, *the cowboy artist,* known for his famous paintings inspired by the area's scenery, people and history. One visit here, and you will understand how one place could inspire a lifetime of paintings.

With its towering mountains, remote forests and rolling plains, this area is incredible. Part of the Bob Marshall Wilderness Complex, the third largest wilderness in the lower forty-eight states, is found here. *The Bob* contains one of the best-preserved mountain ecosystems in the world and is home to many animals including grizzly bears and gray wolves.

6. YELLOWSTONE COUNTRY

Yellowstone Country is located in the south-central part of the state and is home to the city of Bozeman, often referred to as *the most livable place*. This region runs along the northern border of (you guessed it!) Yellowstone National Park. Only 3% of Yellowstone is found in Montana, but we do claim three of the five park entrances. In Yellowstone Country you will find stunning rugged mountains that turn into rolling prairies as you head farther east.

This area is known for all things Yellowstone including geysers, hot springs and spectacular wildlife. Additionally, it is a well-known skiing destination. You will also find it is a great place to get out and hike or explore museums and historical sites.

7. MISSOURI RIVER COUNTRY

*The country we passed today…is
one of the most beautiful plains we
have yet seen, it rises gradually
from the river bottom… then
becoming as level as a bowling
green… as far as the eye can reach.*

– Meriwether Lewis, May 6, 1805

Located in the northeastern corner of Montana,
Missouri River Country is a part of the Great Plains
and includes the town of Sidney. A portion of the
Bakken Shale Play, one of the largest oil
developments in the U.S., is found here. The lucrative
oil production in recent years has caused an economic
boom in the area.

The region is named after the Missouri river, the
longest river in North America. Montana's largest
body of water, Fort Peck Reservoir, is found here.
The reservoir was originally formed here in 1937
when Fort Peck Dam was built across the Missouri
River. Today, it is an excellent fishing spot and holds
over 50 different kinds of fish. This region also holds

23

more than one third of Lewis and Clark's path. You can still follow in their footsteps and much of the land looks the same today as it did in 1805.

8. CUSTER COUNTRY

Located in Southeast Montana, Custer Country is named for the 1876 battle, known as *Custer's Last Stand*, between Custer and the Sioux and Cheyenne Indians. Here you will find the city of Billings, Montana's largest city, and Miles City, the *Cowboy Capital of the World* known for its Bucking Horse Sale. This area is a surprise gem in the lower eastern corner of the state. It is comprised of gently rolling plains and Montana's badlands.

The badlands are known for their dry, bare terrain and exquisite buttes, canyons and spires. It is thought that a great fire once burned this area and exposed the sedimentary rock to years of erosion that in turn created this unique landscape. Not only is it beautiful, many scientifically important dinosaur fossils have been found here.

9. MONTANA IS ONE BIG SMALL TOWN

Turn me loose, set me free
somewhere in the middle of
Montana.

– Merle Haggard

If you come to Montana looking for big cities, you better keep looking. You might be wondering how we even call our big towns cities. Our biggest cities are only considered mid-size cities and they still have a small-town feel. Our most populated city, Billings in eastern Montana, holds just over 100,000 people as of 2019. Missoula is the second biggest with a population of a little over 70,000. Great Falls, Bozeman, Butte, Helena and Kalispell are the only other cities with more than 20,000 people. The rest of the cities have populations below 10,000 people. Many of our small towns are home to less than 100 people. Of Montana's 56 counties, 46 of them are considered frontier counties with less than 6 people per square mile.

You are probably seeing a common trend here. Montana is a huge state and it isn't very densely populated. Even though Montana is the fourth largest state, it is only the 48th most populous (following Alaska and Wyoming). As of 2019, the population for the whole state has reached just 1.07 million.

Yes, we are aware that large cities like Los Angeles have more people in one city than we do in our whole entire state. We love this about our state! We feel like we have the best of both worlds. We love our open space and the freedom to explore the great outdoors. We enjoy that our cities are just big enough to provide us with everything we need like great shopping, excellent medical care and unique entertainment.

I have often heard that Montana is like one big small town- and its true! We may be spread out across 147,042 square miles and there may be some rivalry between towns, but at heart, we are like one big small town. Everyone knows someone or knows someone who knows someone from another Montana town that is willing to help a friend out. I think you too will enjoy exploring our vast open space and will find our small town vibe and friendly folks very welcoming.

10. HOW TO GET HERE AND GET AROUND

Montana is surrounded by Canada to the North, North and South Dakota to the east, Wyoming to the south and Idaho to the west. You can arrive here from any direction by highway or interstate. However, if coming from Canada, you will need to follow the proper procedures for traveling internationally.

By Plane

Montana has five international airports and several small airports offering commercial flights connecting to major hubs every day. Since Montana is such a large state, you will probably want to fly into an airport near the area you wish to visit. In the Northwest corner, Glacier Park International Airport is located in Kalispell and is the closest airport to Glacier National Park. Missoula International Airport is about two and a half hours south of Glacier and just over four hours from Yellowstone National Park. Great Falls International Airport is located in central Montana. Bozeman Yellowstone International Airport is just over an hour from Yellowstone National Park. Billings Logan International airport serves the eastern

27

side of the state. Butte and Helena also have small airports offering a couple of flights per day.

By Train

The only passenger train service in Montana is Amtrak's Empire Builder, which connects Chicago to Spokane. The route follows Montana's high-line, or the northern border of the state. There are twelve stops in Montana including several stops in Glacier National Park.

By Bus

Jefferson Lines offers bus service across the state from Whitefish down to Missoula and all the way to the eastern side of the state along Interstate 90. Additionally, Jefferson Lines has routes in the surrounding states of Idaho, Wyoming and North and South Dakota. You can visit their website to book a trip.

Each larger city in Montana offers public bus transportation. In Missoula, the Mountain Line covers the Missoula valley and is completely free to ride. Bozeman's Streamline also offers zero-fare bus service throughout Bozeman. The Metropolitan Transit System in Billings provides bus service throughout Billings for a fee. Most other larger

Montana cities offer bus service for a fee as well. You might be surprised to know that Glacier National Park also offers a bus shuttle service through the park.

Uber, Lyft and Taxi Services

You will find that the larger cities in Montana offer Uber, Lyft and taxi services. This is a great option for going to and from the airport, getting around town or having a safe ride home after a few drinks. However, if you plan to travel very far this option can quickly become expensive.

By Car

The most convenient way to get around Montana is definitely by personal vehicle. Montana is a vast state and travel destinations may be many miles apart. Routes and schedules limit bus and train travel and Uber, Lyft and taxi services are expensive if you plan to travel long distances. Having your own personal vehicle allows you to come and go as you please and see as much of the *Treasure State* as possible. Drive your own vehicle to Montana or rent a car when you arrive. All larger cities have car rental agencies.

11. WHAT YOU NEED TO KNOW ABOUT DRIVING HERE

When driving in Montana, you are sure to enjoy the beautiful scenery and friendly drivers. You will also probably notice that we have about a million different license plate designs. This is due to Montana's Sponsored Plate Program. This program allows vehicle owners the option to choose a charity to make a yearly donation to when they register their vehicle. In return, the vehicle owner gets to display the charity's uniquely designed license plate. It is a fun program, but it can be hard to decide what cause to support and which design to get.

Driving in Montana is usually a great experience. However, our mountainous roads, wildlife and extreme weather can make for hazardous driving conditions. Montana is one of the deadliest states per capita for drivers. Here are a few tips to keep your Montana driving experience pleasant:

Wear Your Seatbelt

First, always wear your seatbelt. This might sound like a no-brainer, but sadly we lose a lot of people every year in auto accidents because they weren't wearing their seatbelt. Wearing your seatbelt could save your life. Additionally, you could be fined for not buckling up. So just buckle up!

Don't Speed

Second, follow the speed limit. Again, this sounds like a no-brainer, but nothing can ruin your day faster than seeing those flashing lights behind you and getting slapped with a big fine. Keep your eye out for posted speed limits and be sure to follow them.

Don't Drink and Drive

The third no-brainer tip, please do not drink and drive. For years Montana was known as a state where you could crack open a beer as you were driving down the highway. This began to change in 2005 when Montana began to take a stronger stance against drunk driving. However, Montana continues to be one of the worst states for DUIs and DUI deaths. So don't become a DUI statistic. Don't drink and drive and please watch out for drunk drivers on the road.

Don't Drive Distracted

Montana doesn't have a statewide law banning cell phone calls and texting while driving. However, many cities have banned the use of handheld devices while driving. So be aware of this. Being ticketed for this can result in a fine. Besides, it is just not safe to drive distracted.

Watch for wildlife

There is wildlife everywhere in Montana and unfortunately this includes our roadways. Hitting an animal with your car is always sad, but hitting a large animal may be devastating for you, the animal and your car. Many common animal crossing areas will have signs posted, but don't assume these are the only areas where they cross because they can and do cross just about everywhere.

Many Montana roadways have wildlife-sensitive designs. These designs integrate tall fences along roadways with gateways that allow animals to exit the road, but not enter it. They allow animals to cross the road by way of bridges or underpasses. US Highway 93 near Evaro has one of the most extensive wildlife-sensitive designs in North America. If you happen to visit this road, you will see the tall fences along the road and the Animal's Bridge over the highway. It is an excellent design for both the driver and wildlife. However, most roads in Montana do not have this excellent wildlife-sensitive design so keep your eyes peeled.

Road Construction

Once the weather warms and the snow melts, road construction season begins in Montana. This season continues until the ground begins to freeze again. Although it slows traffic and can be a real pain when you are trying to get somewhere, our construction workers have to get a lot of work done in a short amount of time. So expect some delays and pay attention to signs, flaggers and pilot cars. Don't speed through construction zones. Traffic fines in construction zones are doubled in Montana.

You Will Love Our Traffic

If you are from the big city, you will probably laugh at what we consider rush-hour traffic in Montana. We often get frustrated driving through our cities during rush hour, but the delays are actually very minimal. Outside of the city, be aware you could get caught in a *Montana traffic jam.* This occurs when animals block our roads. You could be stuck behind a herd of cattle, a group of big horn sheep or even a family of bears. The best thing to do is be patient and wait until the road is clear.

12. WHAT YOU NEED TO KNOW ABOUT WINTER DRIVING

Winter brings plenty of snow, ice and blizzard conditions to our roadways. Check your route's conditions by visiting mtd511.com or calling 511. You can view live webcams of many roads on the Montana Department of Transportation's website. In very severe weather, roads may be closed altogether.

Be Prepared

It is a smart idea to pack an emergency travel kit with you and plenty of warm winter clothes or blankets. Make sure your tires have good tread and are properly filled. Use snow tires or chains if necessary. Don't forget to have a good ice scraper on hand to clear the ice and snow off your windshield before you head out onto the road. Many people pack sand or kitty litter to pour under their tires if they become stuck in the snow. Also, make sure your windshield washer fluid reservoir is filled with winter fluid that will not freeze in case you need to clear your windshield while you're driving (and you probably will need to).

Driving on Slick Roads

When traveling on snow packed or icy roads, expect to go much slower. Give yourself plenty of room away from other cars in case you or they start to slide. Never use cruise control on icy conditions. Remember that ice can be expected on bridges and in shady spots. Sometimes an invisible thin layer of transparent ice, or black ice, covers the road and makes it very slick. If you are watching the road carefully, you may be able to detect a slightly glossier sheen, but it can be hard to spot.

If you happen to hit ice and slide, do not slam on your breaks! Try to stay calm and let off the gas. You can try gently tapping your breaks and steering the car in the right direction. However, aggressively trying to steer out of the slide can send your car skidding or spinning. If you are going to slide off the road, try to steer your car into whatever will be the least damaging.

Snow Plow Safety and Etiquette

Snowplows move slowly and it might be tempting to pass them. However, you should not pass them unless it is absolutely necessary. Be sure to give the snowplow plenty of room and keep in mind that plow drivers may not be able to see your vehicle.

Remember that snowplows send snow and ice flying. This can create poor visibility when passing. Also, you don't want a piece of ice to fly up and hit your windshield. Just be patient and the snowplow will pull over to let vehicles pass. Also, don't follow too close. They are often spreading sand or deicer behind them.

13. MONTANA WEATHER CAN BE EXTREME AND UNPREDICTABLE: BEST TIME TO VISIT

Montana has four distinct seasons: summer, spring, winter and autumn. Our weather can be rather unpredictable in any season and sometimes we are lucky enough to experience all four seasons in one day (this is a joke…kind of). Montana's landscape changes drastically with each season, creating unique visiting opportunities throughout the year.

Summer
Most people would probably say that summer is the best time to visit Montana, from mid-June through

August. This time is often referred to as tourist season. You will find it is easy to access the higher elevations since the snow has melted and most tourist destinations will be open.

Summertime in Montana is gorgeous! You will see hillsides dotted with exquisite wildflowers and snowcapped mountains on the horizon late into the season. The once ice-covered rivers and lakes become sparkling retreats to beat the summer heat. Wildlife is abundant and active. This is the perfect time for outdoor adventures and wildlife viewing.

Temperatures are usually warm and comfortable during the summer. You can expect temperatures in most areas of Montana to reach into the upper 80s during the day. However, we often experience heat waves with temperatures in the 90s and even 100s for short amounts of time. Nights are cooler and can drop down into the 40s and 50s. Higher elevations are generally cooler than the valleys.

Summers are usually fairly dry with occasional afternoon thunderstorms. Sometimes the storms can be intense with high winds, lightning and hail. Montana even sees the occasional tornado, usually on the far eastern side of the state.

The only down side to visiting during the summer is this is when everyone else is visiting too. So attractions can be busy and lodging rates can be expensive. However, even when Montana is crowded, it's still not as crowded as the more populated areas of the United States.

The Shoulder Season

You may be able to avoid some of the crowds and save some money by planning your trip in the shoulder season, which includes early June and September. However, planning your trip at this time can be a gamble if you plan to visit higher-elevations. You could encounter snow and cooler weather during this time. Sometimes high-elevation roads, such as the Going to the Sun Road in Glacier National Park, aren't even open until mid-June or early July and can close as early as September.

Autumn

The autumn months of September and October are always beautiful in Montana. This is actually my absolute favorite Montana season! The air becomes crisp and the trees take on vibrant hues of yellow, orange and red. We often wake up to brisk mornings with frost on the ground. By afternoon, the sun melts off all the frost and the temperatures often reach into the 50-70 degree Fahrenheit range.

It can be a great time to explore Montana when it is less busy and before the snow falls. However, keep in mind we sometimes get early snowstorms at this time. Other times we luck out and experience a long Indian summer with beautiful blue skies and plenty of sunshine.

Winter

> *What good is the warmth of summer, without the cold of winter to give it sweetness.*

– John Steinbeck

Winter is often overlooked as a good time to travel to Montana. However, it can be an incredible time to visit. Winter dramatically transforms Montana's landscape into a magnificent winter wonderland. The pristine white snow contrasts beautifully with our bluebird skies.

In the higher elevations, you might be lucky enough to encounter our mysterious *snow ghosts*. They sound spooky, but they are actually quite spectacular. These snow-laden trees stand out eerily from the white powder like mystical snow creatures.

They are actually formed by rime ice sticking to the trees. They are basically hard pillars of ice (so don't run into them).

When visiting during winter, you can expect freezing temperatures and plenty of snowfall. Traveling in most high elevations can become difficult, if not impossible. Most of the snow falls between November and March, but it is not uncommon to have snow in the higher elevations from September to May.

High in the Rocky Mountains on the western side of the state we can get up to 300 inches (yes, that is 25 feet!). In Eastern Montana the average is about 20 inches of snow. Most of our larger cities receive between 30 to 50 inches. Remember that the snow often melts off and on throughout the winter so we rarely will have that much on the ground at one time.

Winter is an excellent time to visit if you enjoy skiing, snowshoeing or snowmobiling. Montana has excellent ski resorts! Winter is also a great time to rent a cabin, cozy-up by the fire and enjoy the views of the winter wonderland outside. Perhaps test out your ice-skating skills or take a ride on a horse-drawn sleigh.

Spring

Spring begins in April and can run through early June. Winters in Montana can be great, but they can be long. You might see us running around outside in short-sleeves and shorts at the first sign of spring. We know it is still cold, but we are just so excited. Plus, after braving freezing temperatures for months, that first warm day feels pretty warm to us.

In the spring, we usually see plenty of rainfall that can last until July. The temperatures begin to warm and usually reach the mid-70's by late May or early June. The high elevation snowpack begins to melt and fills our rivers and streams, making them high, fast and sometimes dangerous. We usually experience some flooding. And there's mud. So much mud. Everywhere.

Lodging rates are usually low at this time and you won't have to deal with many crowds. This can be an exciting time for wildlife viewing because many animals give birth to their young in the spring and bears begin to emerge from hibernation. However, trails and mountain roads are often muddy or impassible and many tourist attractions are not yet open.

Extreme Weather

Montana is known for extreme and unpredictable weather. We hold the record in the United States for the greatest temperature change in 12 hours. In Fairfield on December 14, 1924, the weather dropped from 63 degrees Fahrenheit to negative 21 degrees Fahrenheit in 12 hours. This is an 84-degree change! We also hold the record for the coldest temperature in the contiguous United States. On January 20, 1954, the temperature was recorded at negative 70 degrees Fahrenheit on Roger's Pass (Brrr!!).

The changing weather in Montana can be incredible. However, these extreme changes can be dangerous if you don't know what to expect. Always be prepared! Be sure to check the local weather forecast and be aware of any weather alerts.

Local news and radio stations broadcast weather alerts, as does the Montana Department of Transportation. Some apps that can be helpful are NOAA Weather Radar Live, AccuWeather and MDT Travel Info. Montana Weather Authority is also a great app. It is full of useful weather information and it shows current forecasts, alerts and road condition maps.

14. FIRE SEASON AND SAFETY

Only you can prevent wildfires.

– Smokey Bear

As summer progresses, Montana begins to experience another season, the dreaded fire season. Nothing ruins a gorgeous Montana summer worse than a bad fire season. If there is ever a time when Montanans want to leave our state, it is during a bad fire season. Fortunately, this doesn't occur every year.

By August (and sometimes as early as July), Montana's snowpack has mostly melted and the summer heat coupled with little precipitation creates a very dry environment that is primed for forest fires. These fires can become huge, destructive forces that burn through forests and even homes. The smoke can encompass an area for weeks, making for poor visibility, breathing issues and overall low morale. It can be miserable. Firefighters often cannot put the fire out so they work to control it.

When traveling in Montana during fire season, be aware of where the wildfires are located. A bad fire can shut down an entire area and you could have to change your travel plans. In August 2017, Glacier National Park was partially closed due to the lightning-caused Sprague Fire that burned the Sperry Chalet.

However, Smokey Bear was right, you CAN prevent wildfires (or forest fires as the former slogan proclaimed). We can work together to help prevent fires and keep Montana an enjoyable place. We can't stop lightning-caused or other naturally occurring fires, but there are many things we can do to prevent human-caused fires.

Roasting s'mores over a roaring campfire under the beautiful night sky is almost a Montana right of passage. However, campfires can cause wildfires so be sure to follow proper safety precautions. When the fire danger is high, burning is not allowed. So check the restrictions before starting any kind of fire. They are usually posted in campgrounds or visit firerestrictions.us.

When preparing your campfire, a designated fire pit is always preferred. However, if you have to build your own pit, start by digging a pit and circling it with rocks. Make sure the ground is cleared down to the dirt 10 feet around your pit and that there are no branches above it. You must keep a bucket of water and shovel near the fire. Never leave your fire unattended.

When you are done with your fire, it is important that you put it completely out. Dump plenty of water on the fire and stir it with a shovel. Then dump more water on it. Continue this process until it is cold.

Just driving down the road, your vehicle could cause a spark that ignites a wildfire. Make sure nothing is dragging from your vehicle such as broken parts or towing chains. Be sure your tire pressure is good because wheel rims hitting the ground can cause sparks. Don't drive through tall grass and NEVER throw cigarette butts on the ground.

15. MONTANA'S DRESS CODE: CASUAL AND PRACTICAL

When you picture Montana fashion, you might picture a cowboy dressed in the cliché cowboy attire complete with blue jeans, a big belt buckle, boots and a cowboy hat. While it is true that western wear never goes out of style in Montana, keep in mind that Montanans can spot an imposter cowboy from a mile away. So if you show up wearing head-to-toe brand new cowboy apparel you are going to stand out like a sore thumb.

Not all Montanans dress like cowboys and cowgirls. In fact, on any given day in Montana you will see people dressed in all kinds of styles including sportswear, trendy fashions and plain old casual jeans and t-shirts. Montanans, as a whole, tend to lean towards casual and practical attire. Many Montanans spend a good amount of time working and recreating outdoors so weather-appropriate clothing is always important. We do dress up for special occasions, but for most events or nice dinners your best jeans and a nice shirt are perfect.

When visiting Montana, come casually dressed, but remember to dress practically. Keep the weather and your planned activities in mind and dress accordingly. Remember that weather in Montana can vary drastically so check the forecast and come prepared. It is a good idea to dress in layers so you can easily adjust to changing weather.

16. STAYING CONNECTED: INTERNET AND CELL SERVICE

Next time you turn off a news cycle filled with shouting bobble heads convinced that America is devolving into a demonic inferno, maybe you should come here.

– Anthony Bourdain

Our state is vast and it is not very densely populated. So there are many areas in Montana where it doesn't make sense money-wise for cell-phone companies to put in cell-phone towers. Because of this, there are many rural and mountainous regions throughout Montana where you will not have cell service. If you plan to be out of the coverage area and feel you will need access to a phone, you can rent a satellite phone. Check with your cell phone provider or other satellite phone rental company for rates.

However, all big cities, most small towns and most major highways will have cellular service. You will also find Internet access in all cities and most small towns. Most hotels, coffee shops, airports and libraries will also have free Wi-Fi access.

In more remote areas, you might feel like you've gone back in time when you don't have Internet access and the only option for a phone call is a landline or satellite phone. However, Montana is truly a great state to disconnect from your computer or phone and reconnect with yourself, your family or the great outdoors. You might find it refreshing to set your devices down and truly be present in the moment, taking in the beauty and peace that Montana offers.

17. TRAVELING WITH PETS

Montana can be an excellent place to travel with your fury friends. We have plenty of open space, excellent hiking trails and plenty of fresh clean water to play in. There are many hotels, rental homes and campsites that welcome pets. Most large cities have great off-leash dog parks and many restaurants and breweries allow dogs on their outdoor patios (be sure to check ahead of time). Just walking down the sidewalks, you will see that many businesses set out water dishes for pups during the hot summer.

Dogs are welcome at almost all of Montana's state parks except Frenchtown Pond, Wild Horse Island, Smith River and Spring Meadow Lake (during the summer months). Your pet must be kept on a leash that is less than 8 feet long. Be sure to properly dispose of your pet's waste. Don't let your dog bark excessively or dig up the ground and keep your pets away from wildlife.

Visiting Glacier National Park with a pet is allowed. However, there are many restrictions. Pets cannot be on trails, lakeshores, in the backcountry or in buildings. They also cannot ever be left tied up or unattended. They are allowed in developed campgrounds, picnic areas, on boats on the lake, beside roads and in parking areas. They must be on a leash that is less than 6 feet long at all times. If they are in the back of a truck, they must be restrained. The only trail that dogs are ever allowed on is the bike trail from Apgar to West Glacier.

Service animals that meet ADA requirements are allowed in Glacier. However, it is recommended that you register your service animal at the visitor center or ranger station. It is not recommended to take a service animal in the backcountry. Doing so could set you and your pet up for a confrontation with a wild animal.

As you can see, taking a dog or pet to Glacier really restricts your activities. The rules are practically identical for Yellowstone National Park. There are several kennels near both parks where you could board your pet while you enjoy the park. Be sure to make arrangements in advance because they can fill up fast.

EXPERIENCE THE BEST OF MONTANA

18. GREAT PLACES TO STAY IN MONTANA

Montana has an abundance of wonderful overnight accommodations. You will find that our cities and towns have many hotels and motels ranging from unique independent businesses to well-known chains. For a truly unique Montana experience, here are my top picks:

Rent a Vacation Home or Cabin

Renting a Montana vacation home or cabin can make you feel right at home and you can live like a local while you're here. There are many homes to choose from ranging from rustic to extravagant. You could rent a remote cabin, small condo or sprawling lakeside estate.

If you are traveling in a group, your whole group could stay in one location and you could save money by splitting the cost. You could cook your own food if you want and most have on-site laundry. Many are also pet friendly. Some located near lakes even offer boats or kayaks for you to use. You really have the opportunity to choose a rental that best suits your needs. You will find Montana vacation rentals listed on most well known vacation rental websites.

Stay in a Charming Bed and Breakfast

Montana has many unique bed and breakfasts throughout the state including many with interesting histories. Staying at a B&B can give you the opportunity to meet other travelers and your host may give you unique insight into the area. Plus, who doesn't love waking up to a home-cooked breakfast. The Montana Bed and Breakfast association is an excellent resource to find your perfect bed and breakfast accommodations.

Luxury Dude Ranches and Glamping

Montana has some amazing dude ranches that allow you to truly experience Montana at its finest. Whether you are looking for a wilderness escape or want to experience the cowboy life, Montana has you covered. If you love the idea of camping, but need something a little more glamorous then glamping is for you. It is almost impossible to choose because there are so many great options, but here are my favorites:

- **Triple Creek Ranch**

Located in the Bitterroot Mountains near Darby, Triple Creek Ranch is a luxury ranch resort for adults. The ranch offers private cabins and ranch homes. Here you can enjoy gourmet cuisine and activities such as horseback riding, archery or fly-fishing.

- **The Ranch at Rock Creek**

The Ranch at Rock Creek is an all-inclusive ranch on a 19th century homestead near Philipsburg. You can choose to stay in a luxury home, in the lodge, in the historic barn or a glamping cabin. You can enjoy being pampered in the spa or enjoy a hike or wagon ride.

- **The Resort at Paws Up**

Just outside of Missoula, the Resort at Paws Up is one of the best resorts in the Rocky Mountains. It is a working Montana ranch that offers luxury homes and glamping accommodations complete with a butler. You can participate in cattle drives, outdoor adventures and several delicious dining experiences. It also has great activities for kids.

Enjoy a Wonderful Stay in a Montana Resort

- **Chico Hot Springs Resort and Day Spa**

Chico Hot Springs is located in the Paradise Valley near Yellowstone National Park. It was established in 1900 and offers 152 acres for outdoor adventures, two mineral hot pools and a western saloon. You can stay in the historic main lodge or in their private log homes, cabins or chalets.

- **Whitefish Mountain Resort**

Whitefish Mountain Resort is a ski resort located in the town of Whitefish near Glacier National Park. In the winter, enjoy excellent skiing and in the summer enjoy zipline tours, downhill mountain biking and the Aerial Adventure Park. It also is home to Montana's only alpine slide. They offer many great lodging options.

Camping

Camping in Montana is popular with locals and tourists alike, and for good reason. It is generally a low-cost activity that allows you to get up close and personal with nature. Camping is a great way to disconnect from technology and live in the moment. You can connect with family or friends or relax in solitude. Not to mention, it is really fun!

When camping in Montana, you can choose from backcountry camping, primitive campgrounds or full-service campgrounds. You could park your RV, sleep in a tent or even camp out under the stars. For some unique camping adventures check out Somers Yurt near Flathead Lake, Lodgepole Gallery and Tipi Village on the Blackfeet Indian Reservation or stay in Shepherd's Covered Wagon at the Virgelle Merc Antiques and Accommodations along the Missouri River.

Truly Unique Accommodations
- **Snow Bear Chalet**

The Snow Bear Chalet is located on Hope Slope at Whitefish Mountain Ski Resort and is comprised of three treehouse chalets. You can ski in and out from the tree houses. You can even relax in your private hot tub on the deck as you watch the skiers on the slopes.

- **Cougar Peak Lookout**

You can stay in an old-time Forest Service fire lookout on top of the Cabinet Mountains. It can accommodate four people. There is no water, but there is a rustic outhouse. It is truly a one-of-a-kind experience with unbelievable mountain views.

- **The Shire of Montana**

The Shire of Montana is modeled after the Hobbit houses from J.R.R. Tolkien's *Lord of the Rings*. It is located in the Cabinet Mountains and has been named as one of the ten best movie themed hotels in the world. It is a one-of-a-kind experience. However, you must be twelve or older to stay here.

19. EAT LIKE A LOCAL– SEVEN THINGS TO TRY PLUS DESSERT!

Food is everything we are. It's an extension of nationalist feeling, ethnic feeling, your personal history, your province, your region, your tribe, your grandma. It's inseparable from those from the get go.

– Anthony Bourdain

When you think of Montana, food destination might not be the first thing that comes to mind. However, folks from the Treasure State know that Montana is truly a culinary treasure trove. Here in *Big Sky Country*, we are fortunate to enjoy locally raised grass-fed beef, wild game, locally grown fresh produce and delectable wild edibles. You will find that there are many great places to sample Montana cuisine including farmers markets, roadside stands, food-trucks, hole-in-the wall cafes and gourmet restaurants.

Growing up in a family-owned restaurant in a small Montana town, I was fortunate to see firsthand how food brings people together. It is a language we all speak. Locals and visitors alike loved sharing their stories at my family's restaurant over a delicious bowl of our dear family friend, Ginny's, Old Fashioned Tomato Soup or one of my grandma Flora's famous cinnamon rolls.

It was hard work to keep the restaurant afloat, but the bond shared with others helped to make it worthwhile. Our customers became our friends. If you have to choose between a chain restaurant and a local restaurant during your Montana visit, I strongly recommend you eat local. Not only are you supporting a local business, but you also will enjoy an authentic Montana culinary experience and you might even make friends with the locals.

Here are a few things you should try while you're here:

Elk, Bison and Beef

If you are a meat eater, Montana is the perfect place for you! (Don't worry if you don't eat meat-Montana is becoming more vegetarian and vegan friendly every day.) Montana is well known for the high quality cattle and bison our ranchers raise. We are also known for our wild game. And boy do we ever know how to grill up a delicious steak or burger! Many restaurants serve local beef and bison or even wild game such as deer or elk.

Lolo Creek Steakhouse is one of my favorites! Located near Missoula in the small town of Lolo, this log cabin steakhouse offers delicious food and an authentic Montana experience. It was even recognized by Food Network as one of the 50 best steakhouses in the US. The grill masters cook the steaks over a wood-fired grill in the middle of the dining room. You can literally hear the sizzle and smell the delicious aroma of your steak as it cooks. Their signature rib-eye steak is fantastic. Seating is first-come-first-serve so there can be a wait. Fortunately, the bar offers delicious drinks and cocktails. Additionally, the steakhouse is right next to the Lolo Creek Distillery and Tasting Room.

Montana also makes some delicious jerky. Check out Hi-Country Jerky if you are near Lincoln. Their products are sold throughout the state, but High Country's Trading Post Retail Store in Lincoln is always a neat stop. It is full of their meat snacks as well as other local Montana foods and Montana art, jewelry and clothing. It is also home to the Upper

Valley Historical Society. You can view artifacts from the valley or take a tour of the historical buildings behind the trading post.

On a side note, J. Johnson's Trophy room is also located at the trading post. You can view impressive wild-game trophy mounts. Many are full-size and give you a great idea of what the animal looks like up close and personal. Speaking of mounts, if you visit the trading post, you must visit the Lincoln Ranger District Office to see one of Montana's largest grizzly bears. He was 12 years old and 830 pounds when a truck on Highway 200 tragically struck him. Many taxidermists donated their time to create a beautiful mount. One look at his sheer size (and those claws!) and you will have a deepened respect for the bears in our forests.

Pasties

Pasties (pronounced past-ees) were originally introduced to the mining city of Butte in the 1800s, likely by Cornish immigrant miners. These meat and vegetable pies were filling and handy (Literally, they were held in the hand and didn't need a dish). They were also delicious and cheap to make.

Today this miner's meal has become a Montana favorite. There are many great recipe variations, but

59

in general all recipes call for ground beef, potatoes, onions and sometimes carrots tucked inside of a pastry. They are often served covered in brown gravy. Check out the *Butte Heritage Cookbook* for a great authentic recipe. You can find many delicious recipes online as well.

There are many excellent places to enjoy a pasty. Nancy's Pasty Shop and Catering in Butte is a great choice, but be warned they are big (1.25 pounds!). Joe's Pasty Shop is excellent and has been featured on the Travel Channel. They have used Joe's original recipe since 1947. They also offer a pasty variation smothered in chili, cheese and onions. Outside of Butte, there are many great places to find pasties including Lisa's Pasty Pantry in Missoula and Wind's Pasties in Anaconda.

Rocky Mountain Oysters

What is a Rocky Mountain oyster you ask? Well, many Montanans consider these oysters a delicacy. To put it bluntly, Rocky Mountain oysters are deep-fried bull testicles. Generally, they are skinned and pounded flat. Then they are coated in flour, pepper and salt, deep-fried and served as an appetizer. However, you might find slightly different variations. It is important to note that ranchers castrate cattle so they don't reproduce and not simply for this unique culinary dish.

Thrillist.com lists the rocky mountain oyster as Montana's top bar food on their list, *The Unofficial Bar Snack of Every State*. However, they aren't found in most of our bars throughout the state. If you get a hankering to try a Rocky Mountain oyster, visit Stacey's Old Faithful Bar in Gallatin Gateway, the Old Saloon in Emigrant or Bull Mountain Grille in Billings.

Many local communities and ranchers get together for Rocky Mountain oyster feeds. It isn't uncommon for ranchers to grill them up fresh after a branding. Up until recently, you could attend the infamous Testicle Festival for a wild time and plenty of Rocky Mountain oysters. However, after thirty-five years, the festival has ended.

Flathead Cherries

Along the crystal clear waters of Flathead Lake, you will find thriving cherry orchards. Cherries don't grow everywhere in Montana. However, Flathead Lake offers the perfect growing conditions with just the right climate and an abundant glacier-fed water supply.

In May the blossoms on the cherry trees create a spectacular scene along the sparkling lake. By July, the cherries are deep red and ripe for picking. Cherries sold before July are likely from out of state. The Flathead area usually produces 3-5 million pounds of cherries each year, but has produced as much as 7 million pounds.

Many orchards offer a pick-your-own option. You can also find roadside fruit stands all around the lake. Stores (local and as far away as California or Ohio) and farmers markets will be selling flathead cherries. The Polson Main Street Flathead Cherry Festival in July is a fun event where you can sample Flathead cherries, check out locally made food and art or compete in a cherry pie-eating contest or cherry pit-spitting contest.

Morel Mushrooms

Morels are very popular in Montana in late spring and early summer. They taste great and often grow abundantly. They are easier to identify than many mushrooms due to their spongy-looking cap. They can be black, white/gray or golden/yellow. They are a delicious wild treat, but they should always be cooked before eating. They are great fried in butter.

Mushroom hunting can be a fun activity. Areas burned by wildfire are usually prime growing spots for morel mushrooms. Mushroom hunters can become territorial if they find a good location so be sure to give others plenty of space and don't expect anyone to tell you where to find them. Make sure you know how to properly identify a morel. There are morel lookalikes that can be deadly or make you sick.

Also, check out the regulations regarding forest product permits. You can find them on the Forest Service website or stop by a Forest Service office. You are allowed to pick up to one gallon of mushrooms in national forests without a permit and up to five gallons per season. They have to be cut in half from root to cap to prevent commercial sale. If you plan to pick more or want to sell them then you will need a permit. If you don't feel like picking your own, almost all farmer's markets will have an excellent supply early in the season.

Huckleberries

Ahhh…huckleberries, one of Montana's most delicious wild treasures. These little purple berries grow in mountainous regions from Wyoming to Alaska. In Montana, they are found more on the mountainous western side of the state and especially near Glacier National Park.

They are very hard to tame so nearly all huckleberries are foraged in the wild, making them rare and often expensive. You will find huckleberry everything in stores and gift shops throughout the state. You can find huckleberry honey, jam, wine, candles, soaps and much more. Check out the Huckleberry Patch in Hungry Horse, the unofficial *Wild Huckleberry Capital of the West*, located near the west entrance of Glacier. There are also many excellent locally made huckleberry pies, pastries and ice cream. The huckleberry bear claws at the Polebridge Mercantile and Bakery located on the west side of Glacier are incredible.

These products are all amazing! However, you really have to try a freshly picked huckleberry. Local farmer's markets and some stores will carry fresh huckleberries usually later into the summer (around August). You can also find them frozen.

If you are here during huckleberry season, you can pick your own. The hardest part is finding a good huckleberry patch. Once you find your berry patch, its time to get to picking. Be ready for your fingers to turn purple. Hopefully you can stop yourself from eating them faster than you can pick them. You won't need a permit unless you plan to pick more than ten gallons or if you want to sell them. Lastly, remember that bears love huckleberries too so always be bear aware.

Wheat and Grains

Montana produces a great deal of wheat and grain. In fact, we come in third out of the US states for our wheat production. The Wheat Montana Farms near Three Forks grows some of the highest quality wheat and grain in the world. They clean and process the wheat and grain and produce flour on-site. They sell their flour, grains and cereal locally as well as nationwide. They utilize their crop in their on-site bakery where they bake up some of the best non-GMO breads, buns and bagels.

A fun fact for you: In September 1995, Wheat Montana broke the Guinness Book of World Records record for the fastest field to loaf (microwave). They produced 13 loaves of bread from wheat that was growing in the field. It took them 8 minutes 13.6 seconds and they used 13 microwaves.

You can visit their Wheat Montana Bakery and Deli locations in Three Forks, Great Falls, Kalispell and at two locations in Missoula. They offer a wide variety of tasty sandwiches made on their freshly baked bread, delicious breakfast options including Wheat MT 7-grain oatmeal and hearty soups. They also sell fresh bakery items. You have to try their (huge!) cinnamon rolls. They are the best!

Sweet Treats

If you have a sweet tooth, Montana has you covered. We have many options for you to choose from. You will love our locally made ice creams including Big Dipper Ice Cream (Missoula and Helena), Wilcoxson's Ice Cream (Livingston), and Sweet Peaks Ice Cream (Whitefish and Missoula). Each one provides a unique flavor, but they all often feature local specialty flavors like huckleberry.

We also have fantastic bakeries serving custom cakes and desserts. Some great bakeries to try are Sweet Pea Bakery in Bozeman, Black Cat Bake Shop and Bernice's Bakery in Missoula and JJ's Bakery in Great Falls. Also, don't forget about our candy shops. Here are two of my favorites:

The Sweet Palace in Philipsburg is an incredible candy emporium located in a beautiful reclaimed building that was once a hardware store. You can choose from over a thousand candies, including sugar free candies. They also make every kind of fudge you could imagine as well as chocolates, truffles, marshmallows and salt-water taffy. You can watch the salt-water taffy being made behind the counter as you pay. There is something for everyone here. However, you should know they are closed on Saturdays.

The Parrot Confectionary Store in Helena originally opened in 1922. Locals know that this is the place to go for homemade specialty candies and chocolate. Many are made from recipes more than 100 years old. When you walk into The Parrot, you will immediately notice that it looks just like an old-fashioned soda fountain. It is virtually unchanged since 1938. In addition to candy, they also serve delicious milkshakes, homemade soda, sundaes and even chili.

20. WHAT TO DRINK– BREWERIES, DISTILLERIES AND COFFEE!

Drink heavily with locals whenever possible.

– Anthony Bourdain

As you adventure through Montana, you will undoubtedly get thirsty. Montana's many sparkling rivers and streams can look tempting with their crystal clear waters. However, as with most outdoor streams, they are not suitable for drinking. Rather, enjoy some of Montana's fresh spring water. Montana Silver Springs out of Philipsburg bottles up some delicious Montana spring water and they ensure it is clean and pure. They also package it in environmentally friendly recyclable aluminum cans.

If you are looking for something with a little more kick than water, Montana offers many other great thirst-quenching options. Montana has many great local cideries, meaderies, wineries, breweries and distilleries (Whew! That's a lot of *ies*!). If you are looking for a caffeine fix, Montana also has many excellent local roasting companies and quirky coffee shops.

Breweries

Montanans love their beer and we have many to choose from. In fact, we have about 85 breweries (and counting!) and we rank second in the US for breweries per capita as of 2019. Historically, breweries have been engrained in our way of life since the first brewery, Thorn-Smith Brewery, was formed in 1863 back when Montana was still a territory.

Today, Montana continues to be a first-rate location for beer production. Brewers source most of their ingredients locally. We have the climate and land to grow excellent wheat and barley and right next door we have Pacific Northwest hops. High quality and specialized craft malts are made right in Montana. We also have plenty of fresh clean water. Combine high quality locally sourced ingredients with expert know-how and you get award-winning Montana brews.

Local Montana breweries are the perfect place to sample our beers and meet the locals. The Montana Brewers Association puts out a fun trail map of the breweries across the state. The Montana Brewery

Passport is another fun booklet made to look similar to a passport. It lists all of Montana's breweries and you can collect stamps from each brewery that you visit. Montana is always adding new breweries so you can download blank expansion pages online to add to your passport. The passport can be purchased online or in many gift shops. Share your adventures online using the tag #MTBrewPassport or on the Montana Brewery Passport Facebook page.

Distilleries

If you are looking to sample something a little stronger, Montana has several high-quality distilleries producing award-winning spirits. Check out the Montana Distiller's Guild for a list of local distilleries to visit. A tour of a Montana craft or farm distillery is always fun and informative and usually includes a spirit tasting. Be sure to call ahead to check the tour availability.

Brewery and Distillery Festivals

Montana holds several brewfests and distillery festivals throughout the year. These festivals are usually listed on the Montana Distiller's Guild and Montana Brewer's Association websites as well as advertised locally. These are great opportunities to mingle with the locals and sample a wide variety of Montana's exceptional local craft beers and spirits.

Coffee

You will find no shortage of delicious coffee in Montana. We have dozens of specialty coffee roasters and even more charming coffee shops. It is so hard to choose a favorite because there are so many superb options. However, according to *Food & Wine* magazine, the best Montana coffee of 2019 is found at Treeline Coffee out of Bozeman. This roasting company is unique because the coffee is grown by women, imported by women and roasted by women. It is also delicious. My personal favorite Montana coffee comes from Black Coffee Roasting Company out of Missoula. There are many, many more great choices across the state. It doesn't matter where you are in Montana; you are usually never very far from a delicious cup of locally roasted coffee.

21. GLACIER NATIONAL PARK– THREE INCREDIBLE ADVENTURES

If this isn't God's backyard, then
He certainly lives nearby.

– Robin Williams

Glacier National Park is a place unlike any other. Glacier's beauty is otherworldly with dramatic peaks, lush green forests and gorgeous alpine meadows dotted with wildflowers and bear grass. The glacial water flows down mountainsides and over spectacular waterfalls where it fills the lakes and streams with pristine blue water in the most stunning shades of turquoise. Glacier is untamed and wildlife including grizzly bears, mountain goats and wolverines roam freely. Visiting Glacier is an impressive, if not spiritual, experience. It is a place you really have to see to believe.

Glacier is named for the strong glacial ice flows that carved the valleys and shaped the massive granite peaks more than two million years ago. Today there are still more than two-dozen glaciers in the park.

This massive park holds more than a million acres and is home to 20 different species of trees, almost 70 species of mammals and more than 270 species of birds. The park offers more than 700 miles of hiking trails, allowing humans to delve right into this beautiful land. It would take a lifetime to experience all this park has to offer. Here are a few must-sees:

Going to the Sun Road

You can't visit Glacier without driving the Going-to-the Sun Road! Literally, you almost can't because it is the main road through the park, but you shouldn't miss it either because it is a must-see. This 50 mile scenic drive crosses the continental divide and offers incredible views of waterfalls, glacial lakes and steep mountainsides. There are many interesting spots to pull over and observe the scenery or take a hike.

Keep in mind that the road doesn't open until the snow melts. This usually occurs in June, but has been known to take until July. Also, the road often closes as early as September or mid-October. So you have a small window during the summer months to take this drive.

This two-lane road runs from West Glacier to Saint Mary. Driving it round trip allows you to see the stunning views from both directions. However, it isn't named Going-to-the Sun Road for nothing. You will literally feel like you are up so high that you are headed to the sun. It can be nerve-wracking to look down over the edge of the steep embankment. Additionally, there are hairpin turns and the road is narrow. This intimidates some drivers.

If you prefer to drive close to the mountainside take the drive beginning at Saint Mary heading towards West Glacier. You will hug the side of the mountains the whole time. This is also the best side to experience the Weeping Wall. You can take Hwy 2 and Hwy 89 along the east edge of the park instead of taking the Going-to-the Sun Road twice.

Before your trip, make sure you fuel up your vehicle and pack drinks and snacks as you will be going many miles without a gas station, store or restaurant. Be sure to pack a jacket too. It is often much cooler at the top of Logan Pass. Remember there might be a lot of visitors so the road could be busy. Be patient and give yourself plenty of time. Most importantly, plan to stop and enjoy the incredible sites and don't forget to take pictures.

If you don't want to drive, take advantage of the park's free shuttle service. The buses are air-conditioned and have big windows. The shuttles run approximately every hour from Saint Mary Visitor

Center to Logan Pass and from Logan Pass to Apgar Visitor Center. It is a great way to see the park without driving and it reduces traffic congestion and pollution. Sometimes the shuttles are full and you have to wait for the next one.

You could also take a guided tour on one of Glacier's historic red buses. These vintage 1930s buses, often called *red jammers,* feature roll back tops perfect for taking in the scenery during good weather. The Blackfeet Indian shuttle bus is another great option and offers guided tours through Blackfeet Country and the Going-to-the Sun Road.

Take a Hike!

Glacier is a hiker's paradise! There are trails for every skill level from beginner to backcountry expert. Many hikes can be completed in a day. The rewards at the end of the trail are spectacular and include waterfalls, glaciers and beautiful turquoise glacial lakes. Not to mention, the trails to get there are pretty impressive. Do remember when hiking in Glacier, to practice hiking safety and be aware of bears (more on this later).

The Trail of the Cedars is a favorite hike for beginners because it is one of the easiest trails in the park and it is wheelchair accessible. On this hike, you will follow a boardwalk that meanders through ancient cedars and hemlocks. Due to the humidity in the valley, the cedars can reach up to 200 feet tall and 4 to 7 feet across. You will also see ferns and mosses. This area looks much more like the Pacific Northwest than it does Montana. Other parts of the trail are either paved or mostly flat dirt pathways.

Halfway through the hike you will reach the footbridge over Avalanche Creek. You can watch the crystal blue glacial water as it cuts through lower Avalanche Gorge. For a closer look, you can climb up the short steep trail and watch as the water flows through the narrow gorge. However, the trail isn't wheelchair accessible beyond the footbridge. If you are up for longer hike, Avalanche Lake is only a little ways further up the trail.

Along the trail to Avalanche Lake, you will come across hundreds of fallen trees that were taken down by avalanches. When you reach the lake you can stop and enjoy the beautiful lake scenery. You will notice several waterfalls cascading down the mountainside into the lake. Much of the water in these falls originates from Sperry Glacier. However, the glacier can't be seen from the lake. If you would like to continue on at this point you can continue on the trail to the head of the lake.

Glacier offers many other incredible hikes. With so many choices, it is hard to decide which hikes to go on. I highly recommend planning in advance. Read up on the hikes, decide what you want to see while you are in Glacier and take into account your hiking experience and ability. I have used the website hikinginglacier.com to read up on trails that I have hiked. They have basic information and photos for over 60 hikes and they rate them based on difficulty. They also state that they have personally hiked all of the trails so you know you are getting an accurate overview of the hikes. The National Park Service also has great trail maps.

See a Glacier

When you are in Glacier National Park of course you want to see a glacier. Despite the park's name, you won't see glaciers everywhere you look. In fact, most aren't easy to get to and sadly many are quickly receding. Comparative photos of the park's glaciers from the early 1900s to now really show how massive they once were and how much smaller they have become. Some are gone altogether. In the early 1900s there were over 100 glaciers and today there are only about two-dozen active glaciers. Many people visiting the park want to see the glaciers before they are gone.

Jackson Glacier is the easiest glacier to spot. It can be viewed from the Jackson Glacial Overlook on the Going-to-the-Sun Road. Salamander Glacier can be seen from the road in the Many Glacier area. Grinnel Glacier and Sperry Glacier can both be seen after challenging hikes. However, Sperry Glacier can also be spotted from the much easier hike to Hidden Lake Overlook. There are others as well that you can view.

A park map pinpointing the glaciers is the best way to locate them. It can be hard to tell the difference between snowfields and glaciers. Binoculars can help. Visiting at the end of August and beginning of September is the best time to spot glaciers because most of the winter snow melts by this time and you can see the glaciers better.

A Few Tips

Although Glacier is open year round, summer is the best time to visit because heavy winter snowfall closes down much of the park and makes hiking trails inaccessible. Remember that in the higher elevations snow can come early and not melt until late into the spring. Much of Glacier doesn't open until late June or even early July and parts of the park close down as early as September or October. Keep this in mind when planning your trip.

Lastly, with such a small visiting window and so many people wanting to see the park, lodging fills up fast. If you plan to stay in a park lodge, you should book your stay up to a year in advance. Even if you aren't planning to stay right in the park, book your stay early. Prices in this area can also be expensive during this time. Camping is allowed in the park's 13 campgrounds. Most campsites are first come first serve. However you can reserve spots in a few park campgrounds.

22. VISITING YELLOWSTONE NATIONAL PARK- MONTANA'S THREE ENTRANCES

Montana is situated right next to a supervolcano. The Yellowstone supervolcano has a huge magma chamber, which holds about 250 cubic miles of magma. It is capable of producing an eruption many thousands of times more powerful than Mount Saint Helen's 1980s eruption. An eruption of this size would release magma and volcanic ash, devastating much of the United States. Now that is a little frightening and intense!

Fortunately, scientists have closely monitored Yellowstone for many years and don't expect an eruption of this size any time soon. Scientists can pinpoint three large eruptions in Yellowstone's history, with the last one occurring about 640,000 years ago. Many experts believe that even if Yellowstone did erupt, it would likely produce a smaller eruption rather than a full-blown super eruption. However, the media and *doomsdayers* like to raise fear and claim that the supervolcano is long overdue for a catastrophic eruption.

The hot churning magma below Yellowstone creates the over 10,000 hydrothermal features that the park is so famous for. You can watch geysers erupting, hot springs boiling, mudpots bubbling, fumaroles steaming and hot water flowing over beautiful travertine terraces. You will see brilliant naturally occurring colors around these features created by thermophiles, which are heat-loving microorganisms.

Yellowstone is also known for its beautiful landscape with stunning mountains and at least 45 waterfalls. Yellowstone even has its own Grand Canyon. Many wild animals make Yellowstone home including grizzly bears, wild bison, wolves and elk.

You really can't drive through the park without seeing incredible wildlife.

If you have the chance to visit Yellowstone National Park, you absolutely should! It is a must see! Most of Yellowstone is located in Wyoming. However, Montana does claim 3% of the park and three of the five park entrances: the West Entrance, North Entrance and Northeast Entrance.

West Entrance

The west entrance to Yellowstone is the busiest entrance and is found in the Montana town of West Yellowstone. This town offers many lodging and dining options as well as tourist attractions. You can visit the West Yellowstone Visitor Information Center or the Yellowstone Historic Center to learn more about the area. The Grizzly and Wolf Discovery Center is informative and allows visitors to enjoy close-up views of grizzlies and wolves. You can also enjoy a thrilling zipline adventure at Yellowstone Park Zipline. Keep in mind that many tourist attractions are only open seasonally.

The west entrance will lead you directly to Madison where you can head north or south into geyser basins. The Lower Geyser Basin to the south is Yellowstone's largest geyser basin and includes the

Great Fountain Geyser and Fountain Paint Pot. Don't miss the Grand Prismatic Spring in the Midway Geyser Basin. To the north, you will find Norris Geyser Basin. This is the park's oldest and hottest thermal area.

North Entrance

To enter the park from the north entrance you will exit from Interstate 90 at Livingston. This charming small town was once a railroad town. Today, you will find it has a western vibe and is home to ranchers as well as artists and writers. It is only an hour drive to Yellowstone and it is a great place to stay while visiting the park. There are many unique hotels, bed and breakfasts and vacation rentals. Anthony Bourdain spent time here and was particularly fond of the historic Murray Hotel.

As you follow Highway 89 along the beautiful Yellowstone River, you will pass through Paradise Valley. You will quickly understand how the valley got its name. The scenery is incredible with stunning mountain views, vast grasslands and many western ranches.

The last town you will come to before Yellowstone is Gardiner. This charismatic town has a rough cowboy style as well as a resident elk herd.

You won't find fancy luxury hotels and restaurants here. However, there are several Montana-style lodging and dining options. It is a great place to set up your base camp and enjoy the rustic shops and restaurants when you're not exploring Yellowstone.

As you enter Yellowstone's only year-round entrance, you will come to the iconic Roosevelt Arch. There is a great spot right before the arch to pull over and get a picture. This entrance will lead you to Mammoth Hot Springs, where you can take in the stunning beauty of the Mammoth Hot Springs Terraces. Expect to run into many elk here and be sure to give them their space. This is a great introduction to the spectacular beauty and wonder of Yellowstone.

Northeast Entrance

As you head towards the northeast entrance of Yellowstone, you will enjoy an incredible drive along the Beartooth Highway. This highway was named a National Scenic Byway's All American Road. If you keep your eye out along the drive you can spot the unique glacially-carved pyramid shaped mountain that the Crow Indians named *Bear's Tooth*, which gave name to the mountain range. It is usually open from Memorial Day to Columbus Day. This scenic highway reaches 5,000 feet and the scenery is incredible with massive peaks, alpine lakes and wildflower-covered meadows.

Near Cooke City and Silver Gate you will find the northeast entrance into Yellowstone. These towns are very small, but you will find hotels and dining options in Cooke City. As you head into Yellowstone, you will enter Lamar Valley. This incredible valley is an excellent spot to view Yellowstone's wildlife including bison, bears and elk.

23. THREE UNIQUE MONTANA STATE PARKS

Montana has over fifty state parks for you to visit. Each one offers a unique Montana experience. You can learn about our history and culture, spend a day out on a gorgeous lake or view amazing wildlife. Many offer great campgrounds so you can enjoy the area for more than an afternoon. There are so many great state parks to enjoy, but here are three that I find especially unique:

Giant Springs State Park

Located in Great Falls, Giant Springs State Park is home to Giant Springs, one of the largest freshwater springs in the world. It was originally discovered by Lewis and Clark in 1805 and was declared a state park in 1970. The water from Giant Springs flows into the Roe River, the world's shortest river. The Roe River carries the spring water for just 201 feet before emptying into the Missouri River.

Approximately 156 million gallons of water from the Madison Aquifer fill Giant Springs each day. It takes approximately 26 years for the water to travel from its source in the Little Belt Mountains to the spring. The water has been carbon-dated and is about 3,000 years old. Additionally, the water temperature stays at 54 degrees Fahrenheit year round so it doesn't freeze in the winter.

Giant Springs State Park is the only state park in Montana that is home to a fish hatchery. You can stop by Giant Springs State Fish Hatchery and learn about the fish they raise utilizing water from Giant Springs. Be sure to check out the huge trout in the show pond and have fun tossing food to them. The Giant Springs Visitor Center is also a must see while you are visiting the park. The visitor center is full of wildlife identification and education opportunities. They also display impressive taxidermy mounts of grizzly and black bears.

Giant Springs State Park encompasses over 4,500 acres on both sides of the Missouri River and it has 20 miles of trails for biking and walking. There are four waterfalls within the park, including the spectacular Great Falls, and five hydroelectric dams. It is a great place to fish or just take in the beautiful sites. Pack a picnic lunch and spend a whole afternoon exploring this remarkable park.

Pictograph State Park

Pictograph State Park is an extraordinary historical site five miles south of Billings. It is a National Historic Landmark. The caves in the park feature ancient pictographs that give us insight into the lives of the original humans that inhabited this land. There are three main caves that you can view: Pictograph Cave, Middle Cave and Ghost Cave.

In the early 1900s locals knew of these caves and called them Indian Caves. In the 1930s archeologists conducted a dig spanning several years. They unearthed more than 30,000 prehistoric artifacts (some dating back to 3,000 b.c.). They found many items including bone tools, a carved amulet and pottery shards. They even found evidence of a prehistoric lodge on the terrace below the caves. Nine human skeletons were found. Some of the human bones showed signs of burning and bite marks, which could indicate cannibalism.

The more recent artifacts indicated that the people that lived there were nomadic bison hunters. They found evidence that they hunted the bison with bows and arrows. It is thought that they eventually abandoned the caves and began living in tepees in the 1700s when the horse was introduced to the area.

Native Americans consider the park a sacred site or a vision quest site. The Crow Indians call the caves Alahpaláaxawaalaatuua (Please don't ask me to pronounce that), which means *where there is ghost writing*. They believe that there are two types of writing in the caves: biographical or storytelling writing and ghost or spirit writing.

The spirit writing is unique because it is not visible all the time. Under the right conditions or when the cave becomes wet, the pictographs appear. Scientists believe this is due to minerals accumulating on the limestone and covering the pictographs. Then when the mineral deposits become wet they become transparent, revealing the hidden pictographs. However, the Crow Indians believe it is because spirits created the writings and they are only revealed to certain individuals.

You can take a self-guided tour following the 0.25-mile walking path. Don't venture off the trail because you might run into rattlesnakes and prickly pear cactus. Be sure to stop by the visitor center to learn more about the historic site and to grab a free informational pamphlet. You won't be able to get extremely close to the pictographs so bring binoculars to get a good look. Also, if you give your eyes plenty of time to adjust to the light, you might be able to see more pictographs. Who knows, maybe the spirits will have a message for you.

First Peoples Buffalo Jump State Park

Just 20 minutes outside of Great Falls in Ulm, you will find First Peoples Buffalo Jump State Park. This site is also a National Historic Landmark. The park is built around an incredible sandstone cliff known as the Ulm Pishkum (derived from the Blackfeet word Pis'kun meaning *deep blood kettle*). The cliff stretches a mile across and it is likely the biggest bison jump cliff in the world.

Native Americans used the Ulm Pishkum to hunt bison as far back as 500 AD. The Native Americans carefully orchestrated a system to work together and direct stampeding bison herds over the cliff. The fittest Native American men, the runners, wore animal skins and skillfully lured and directed the bison towards the cliff where they fell to the ground below. Another group of Native Americans waited below with spears to kill the injured bison. Once the animals were killed, the women of the tribes would skillfully skin and butcher the bison. They utilized nearly every part of the bison for food, shelter, tools and clothing. Hardly anything went to waste.

Today you can view the drivelines on top of the cliff. At the base of the cliff, bison bones are buried under the earth and artifacts such as arrowheads can still be found. However, it is illegal to remove them from the park. It is amazing to walk this area and imagine the impressive hunting events that took place here.

The Visitor Center is an excellent stop to learn more about the Native American tribes and how they hunted and utilized the bison. There are great exhibits to view, a full-size bison hide tepee to tour and excellent murals to gain a deeper understanding of the area's tribes and the great hunting events that occurred here. You can even try your hand at throwing an atlatl, an ancient Native American hunting spear. If you are intrigued by buffalo jumps,

Montana has many more jump sites. The Madison Buffalo Jump in Three Forks is a great place to check out.

24. THREE FASCINATING HISTORICAL SITES

Montana has a vibrant history that is worth exploring. There are many great historical sites across the state that give us a fascinating glimpse into the lives of the people (and animals) that inhabited this land long before us. You can learn about the dinosaurs that once roamed this land, the Native American tribes that first called Montana home and the hardworking cowboys and miners who earned their keep here. You can even walk in the footsteps of Lewis and Clark. There are so many great historical museums and sites to visit, but here are three of my favorites:

Pompey's Pillar National Monument
Take a step back in time and visit the only physical evidence of the Lewis and Clark Expedition when you visit Pompey's Pillar National Monument. This

historical monument is located about 25 miles east of Billings. While you are here, visit the Interpretive Center to learn about the expedition and how Sacagawea, with her infant son, guided the group. There is also wonderful information about the native culture and the geography of the area. You can view educational exhibits, read excerpts from Clark's journal and even eat a picnic lunch in a tepee. Then you can follow the concrete Riverwalk to Pompey's Pillar.

On July 25, 1806, Captain William Clark carved his name into the sandstone pillar. He named the pillar Pompy's Tower after his nickname for Sacagawea's baby, which she carried on her back for the 14 months she aided the expedition. Later, the name was changed to Pompey's Pillar. Today, you can view Clark's original signature on the pillar, which is encased in glass to protect and preserve it.

Deer Lodge- A Small Town with Two Must See Historical Sites

Deer Lodge is a small town about 38 miles west of Butte. It doesn't seem too exciting at first glance, but it is actually a great place to visit. It has two historical sites that are worth checking out. Make a day of it and see them both. Pack a picnic lunch or enjoy one of the tasty local restaurants.

First stop, the Grant Kohrs Ranch National Historic Site, also known as Montana's first ranch. Carsten Conrad Kohrs bought the ranch, house and livestock in 1865 from Johnny Grant. After a rough start and the loss of 23,000 head of cattle during a tough winter, Kohrs built the ranch into a successful cattle ranch and earned himself the title, Montana's Cattle King.

Today the ranch continues to raise cattle and you can tour the preserved Victorian ranch house and much of the ranch's ninety structures. There are 26,000 artifacts for you to view. It is a great look into the history of Montana's cattle ranching.

Next, head just down the road for a tour of the Old Montana Prison. As a child, I was sure this prison was actually a castle. One look at it with its towering rock walls and turreted towers and you will understand why. Later, when I toured the inside, I found out it wasn't quite the fancy castle I had imagined. Rather, it is a fascinating place that once held some of Montana's worst criminals from 1871 to the late 1970s.

Today you can enjoy a guided or self-guided tour through the prison. I have enjoyed both. The guided tour is great for your first visit. The guides are informative and you can learn a lot about the prison. The self-guided tour is nice because you can go at your own pace and read the information for each area. The prison is so big and there is so much to see. You could even take the guided tour and then wander through the prison grounds and visit areas you want to spend more time exploring.

A word of caution: many people believe the prison is haunted. I can't say for sure, but I do know that there are areas of the prison that leave you with a very eerie feeling. If you really want to see for yourself, take a late night guided ghost tour through the prison. For another paranormal experience, you can even sign up for a virtual convict lockdown where you will be booked into the prison, given convict clothing and locked in a cell over night. They offer breakfast in the morning. They warn that unexpected things could happen during your stay and that a ghost might even occupy your cell.

The fun doesn't end with the prison tour. The Old Montana Prison Museum Complex has even more Montana history for you to explore, all within walking distance. Check out the Montana Auto Museum, which was listed by USA Today as one of the top ten car museums in the country. You can view over 160 cars from all eras. The Frontier Museum is a great place to learn about and view items used by cowboys, ranchers and frontier people from 1829 to 1900. There are over 300 handguns and rifles for you to check out. Outside the Frontier Museum, take a walk through the old west town of Cottonwood City, a neat life-size replica of a frontier town. Yesterday's Playthings is a fun museum to tour and view children's toys dating back to 1859. There are some really neat collections in this museum. The Powell County Museum is another great museum in the complex where you can learn about the history of the Deer Lodge area. There are so many fascinating things to see at the Old Montana Prison Museum Complex.

Little Bighorn Battlefield National Monument
If you find yourself near Billings, you don't want to miss visiting the Little Bighorn Battlefield National Monument. This national monument serves as an important memorial for the lives lost on both sides in the Battle of the Little Bighorn. It is a great place to honor those that lost their lives and also to reflect on the tumultuous history between the United States and the Native Americans.

The 1876 Battle of the Little Bighorn was a battle for control of the Western Territory. This battle is often called *Custer's Last Stand* because the Sioux and Cheyenne Indian tribes defeated Lt.Col. Custer of the United States Seventh Cavalry Regiment. Despite winning this battle, the Native Americans were ultimately defeated in other battles and forced onto reservations.

When you visit the Little Bighorn Battlefield National Monument, you can walk through the battlefield and observe the somber memorial. Apsaalooke Tours offers guided tours given by Native Americans of the Crow Reservation. The tour takes you to the Reno-Benteen Battlefield where the Battle of the Little Bighorn began and concludes at Last Stand Hill where Custer was defeated. The tour guides do a great job of sharing the history and stories from the battle.

If you are visiting in June you might be able to catch the Battle of Little Bighorn Reenactment. This dramatic reenactment includes over 300 actors, many horses and a large production crew. It is quite spectacular to watch the historic battle unfold. After the show, you can observe living history actors portraying the life of cavalrymen and Native Americans.

25. THREE NATURAL MONTANA WONDERS

From the badlands in the east to the Rocky Mountains in the west, Montana is full of spectacular natural wonders. You can take in the stunning views of the river from the impressive thousand foot cliffs in Bighorn Canyon National Recreation Area or visit Flathead Lake to check out the remnants of an ancient glacial lake. You can find incredible natural wonders in every corner of the state, but here are a few of my favorites:

Quake Lake

When you think of Montana, earthquakes might not be the first thing that comes to mind. However, Montana is the fourth most seismically active state. The Intermountain Seismic Belt runs through the middle of our state and we have between 7-9 earthquakes every day. Most of these are so small we don't even feel them.

However, I was woken from a sound sleep by the 5.8 magnitude earthquake centered near Lincoln, Montana, on July 6, 2017. This earthquake caused some minor damage, but nobody was injured. It was

Montana's largest earthquake in forty years, but it doesn't even compare to Montana's biggest earthquake in recorded history.

The Hebgen Lake earthquake occurred on August 17, 1959, just before midnight near West Yellowstone. This earthquake registered at 7.3 (many places list it as a 7.2-7.5) on the Richter scale and released more than 350 times more energy than the 5.8 earthquake we experienced in 2017.

My grandma Flora, who lived approximately 266 miles away from the epicenter of the Hebgen earthquake, often shares the story of how she was just about to lay down in bed when the mattress came up to meet her in the back. Her dad ran outside of the house in his underwear in a panic to see what was going on. The shaking was violent.

At the epicenter of the quake, approximately 250 campers were peacefully camped out under a full moon in the Rock Creek Campground when a loud roar and violent shaking awoke them. The tremendous power of the earthquake triggered a massive landslide burying people beneath it and creating a dam on the Madison River. The landslide dam formed a new lake, fittingly named Earthquake Lake. The lake is five miles long, 1/3 miles across and 190 feet deep.

Nine and a half miles from the campground, the bottom of Hebgen Lake dropped 19 feet in seconds sending a huge wave and extreme winds into the Hebgen Dam. The dam was damaged, but miraculously it held. Parts of Highway 287 fell into the water and land rose 20 feet in some areas. The powerful earthquake also caused many changes to Yellowstone's thermal features.

At least twenty-eight people lost their lives that night and many could never be recovered. Those that survived were injured and trapped. Help wasn't able to reach them until the next day. A heroic nurse named Mildred "Tootie" Greene had been camping at the campground and tended to them all night and likely saved many lives.

Today you can visit the Earthquake Lake Visitor Center from Memorial Day through mid-September. It is a great place to learn about the powerful earthquake that drastically changed the land as well as the lives of those camping in the Rock Creek Campground. You can view Quake Lake and walk along an interpretive trail and check out marked points of interest. You can also pay your respects at the Memorial Boulder and read through the names of those who lost their lives in the great earthquake of 1959.

Lewis and Clark Caverns

Lewis and Clark Caverns State Park is Montana's first state park and it is truly one of Montana's greatest natural wonders. It is located between Three Forks and Whitehall. The park has a nice campground, great visitor center, gift shop, concessions and an outdoor amphitheater for presentations. The only way to view the caverns is by taking a guided tour.

Despite the cavern's name, Lewis and Clark didn't discover the caverns and they likely never visited them. Native Americans knew about the caves for hundreds of years. In 1882, two men from Whitehall likely discovered the caves, but did not tell many people. Ten years later, two hunters discovered the caves when they saw steam coming out of it. Eventually, in 1937 the caverns were made a state park. However, the park didn't open to the public until 1941.

Today you can choose from several guided tours. There is the Winter Holiday Candlelight Tour offered in December where you can tour the cave holding your own personal covered candle. In the summer, you can take the Classic Cavern Tour, which is considered moderate to difficult and lasts about two hours. The Paradise Tour is easier and lasts just over an hour. The Wild Cave Tour is perfect for someone wanting an introduction to caving. This tour allows visitors to explore the wildest parts of the caverns with headlamps, kneepads and helmets. This tour lasts about three hours and requires a lot of bending and crawling.

I have visited the caverns many times and every time I am in awe of how incredible they are. There are many unique stalactites and stalagmites in the limestone caverns. The guides do an excellent job explaining the cave's history, how it was formed and pointing out neat things to look at.

A couple words of advice: be prepared for a ¾ mile hike to the entrance to the cave. The trail is smooth, but it is steep. It might be hot outside, but it is always cool in the caves so be sure to bring a jacket. Also, be prepared to have to bend and stoop to navigate some of the cavern's tighter spots. The caves are lit, but the tour guides generally turn the lights off for a brief moment to experience the darkness so be prepared for that. It is very dark. Lastly, there are some bats in the cave, but don't worry they shouldn't bother you.

Ringing Rocks of Pipestone

Just down I90 from Lewis and Clark Caverns you will find the Ringing Rocks of Pipestone off of exit 241. This unique site is not very well known, but it is a fun stop that is free and open year round. It can be a little tricky to get to because a portion of the road is steep, narrow and requires 4-wheel drive. When you get there, you will see parking and signs.

When you first walk up to the ringing rocks, they just look like a big pile of rocks. However, if you tap them with a hammer they make distinct ringing sounds of various pitches. There are very few places in the world where rocks will ring when tapped. There are many theories as to why the rocks ring. However, they do not ring when separated from the other rocks. Don't try it out though. Removing any rocks from the stack could ruin this natural phenomenon. Lastly, don't forget to bring a hammer because you will need it to make the rocks ring.

26. EXPERIENCE NATIVE AMERICAN CULTURE

Long before settlers moved to Montana, Native American tribes lived freely on the land that is now Montana. Many tribes followed the bison herds and each tribe had their own customs and beliefs. They fought hard in many battles to preserve their land and way of life, but they ultimately were forced onto reservations.

Today Montana is home to eleven Native American tribes and seven reservations: the Blackfeet Indian Reservation, Crow Indian Reservation, Flathead Indian Reservation, Fort Belknap Indian Reservation, Northern Cheyenne Reservation and Rocky Boy's Indian Reservation. Many Native Americans live on the reservation, but just as many others choose to live off the reservation. Each Native American tribe has preserved their cultural heritage, customs and traditions and they all contribute to Montana's unique culture.

There are many ways you can learn about and experience Montana's Native American culture. Montana has many excellent educational museums you can visit such as the Museum of the Plains

Indians in Browning, the Northern Cheyenne Tribal Museum in Lame Deer and the Fort Peck Assiniboine and Sioux Culture Center and Museum in Poplar.

Some Native American events are open to the public such as many powwows, shinny games and rodeos. The Crow Fair and Rodeo, Milk River Indian Days and Rocky Boy's Annual Powwow are all popular events. Montana's tourism website provides a list of the major Native American events and information about each one. You should also read through the section on powwow etiquette if you plan to attend a powwow.

You can purchase beautiful Montana American Indian art and craftwork throughout Montana. However, be careful and make sure you are buying an authentic Native American Made in Montana product. It is illegal to misrepresent an item as an authentic Native American item, but it does happen. The Department of the Interior has a great flyer that can be found on their website to help shop wisely.

27. EXPERIENCE MONTANA RANCH LIFE

Ranching has been an important way of life for many Montanans dating all the way back to the 1850s when the first large herds of cattle were brought to Montana. As mining took off in the state, so did the demand for beef and more successful cattle ranches began popping up across the state. The image of a cowboy out on the range with his horse is often romanticized, but it was (and still is) very hard work to raise cattle. Montana ranchers had to feed the cattle through snow-covered winters and protect them from disease, the elements and even cattle thieves. Sometimes thousands of cattle died during Montana's brutal winters.

Today many ranches have been passed down in families through the generations and are ran as family businesses. You will see the whole family, even the children, working the ranch. Ranchers in ranching communities are generally very supportive of each other and you will often see the entire community coming together in times of need or to help each other with big cattle events like brandings.

I don't know about other places, but I can say that the cattle I have seen in Montana are treated exceptionally well. Ranchers are some of the hardest working and most compassionate people I have ever met. They work hard to feed, care for and protect their cattle from predators.

During calving season, ranchers sacrifice sleep to be there day and night to help deliver newborn calves in Montana's harsh spring weather. They search for the newborn calves in the freezing weather and bring them into barns to warm them and nurse the sick ones back to health. I have even known many ranchers who have brought the sickest or orphaned calves into their homes to care for them until they are strong enough to be outside. It is more than a job to them. It is a way of life engrained in their very being.

Experiencing life on a working Montana cattle ranch is an extraordinary opportunity. There are many dude ranches, resort ranches and working ranches that you can visit. You could go horseback riding, participate in a cattle drive or just enjoy the ranch life. Check out the Montana Dude Ranch Association website for a complete listing of Montana ranches you can visit.

MONTANA'S HUNTING, FISHING AND WILDLIFE

28. MONTANA'S HUNTING SEASON

Go afield with a good attitude, with respect for the wildlife you hunt and for the forest and fields in which you walk. Immerse yourself in the outdoor experience. It will cleanse your soul and make you a better person.

– Fred Bear

Hunting season in Montana is a big deal. Montana offers large populations of wild game and plenty of land for hunting. Hunting seasons can vary based on species, but generally hunting season occurs in the fall.

If you visit Montana during this time, you will undoubtedly see hunters dressed in camouflage and bright orange with rifles hung on gun racks in the rear

windows of their trucks. You will probably even see a
hunter's kill in the back of a pickup truck. Although it
can look gruesome, don't be alarmed. If you plan to
be in the outdoors during this time, keep in mind that
the hunters are out there hunting too.

Historically, hunting in Montana has been
important to human survival as far back as the Ice
Age when nomads hunted huge mammals with
spears. Native Americans used bows and arrows and
buffalo jumps. Later, guns made hunting more
efficient. However, Montana does still have a bow-
hunting season.

Today, hunting continues to be an important way
of life for many Montanans. Most Montana hunters
hunt for sustenance, but many will have their trophies
mounted and hung on their walls. Many hunters enjoy
the connection they feel with nature and the memories
made with family and friends. They are also able to
provide their family with wild game raised on native
food sources and fresh spring water. Children, as
young as twelve, can get a hunting license and carry
on the tradition after passing an approved hunter
safety course.

If you wish to hunt in Montana, you will need to
familiarize yourself with Montana's hunting
regulations and obtain a conservation license and

hunting license. If you are not from Montana, you will need to get nonresident licenses. Keep in mind that the deadlines for the license applications often occur in the spring so you will need to plan ahead. You can view hunting regulations and apply for a license on the Montana Fish, Wildlife and Parks website.

Additionally, if you are unfamiliar with hunting or Montana hunting, hiring a hunting guide is an excellent idea. You can find all kinds of hunting guides and outfitters online, but I think Montana Outfitters and Guides Association is an excellent resource. Their website allows you to enter your criteria and then it lists all of the Montana outfitters that match your criteria. Remember to be safe and happy hunting!

29. WHAT YOU SHOULD KNOW ABOUT FISHING IN MONTANA

*Many go fishing all their lives
without knowing that it is not the
fish they are after.*

– Henry David Thoreau

The beautiful Blackfoot River inspired Norman
Maclean's semi-autobiographical book, *A River Runs
Through It*. Robert Redford's 1992 film adaption of
the book, starring Brad Pitt, introduced the world to
our state's beautiful rivers and excellent fly fishing.
The film was actually filmed on the Gallatin River
due to the industrial pollution and overfishing of the
Blackfoot. However, today after much work, the
Blackfoot river has been restored and is a naturally
functioning, healthy river. Nevertheless, the book and
film have inspired many to come to our state and try
their hand at fly-fishing.

Many of my best memories growing up were the
early mornings I spent fishing with my grandpa Jerry.
We would be at the water as the sun came up. I loved
the mist that would hang above the water and seemed

to glow in the early morning sunlight. To me it was a magical place only made more magical by my grandpa's stories about the Montana he knew. He taught me to fish, but really he taught me so much more than that. I will always treasure my memories of being his fishing buddy, of learning to fish and the beautiful Montana lakes and streams that brought us together.

Montanans and visitors alike enjoy fishing in Montana's crystal clear lakes, rivers and streams that are stocked with more than 85 species of fish. Folks enjoy fly-fishing, worm and bobber fishing, spin fishing and even ice fishing. Fishing is a fun activity and great way to connect with nature. Not to mention, fresh caught fish can be pretty tasty.

If you are coming from out of state, you will need to obtain a Montana conservation license and a fishing license. Also, obtain a copy of the most recent Fish, Wildlife and Parks Montana Fishing Regulations booklet and familiarize yourself with Montana's fishing rules. You can get your license online or at almost any sporting goods store.

Lastly, if you plan to fish on any of Montana's Indian Reservations, you will need to obtain a fishing license from the specific reservation you plan to fish on. You will also need to review the reservation's specific fishing regulations. These licenses can be purchased at most sporting goods stores on the reservation.

30. WILDLIFE VIEWING TIPS

Look deep into nature, and then you will understand everything better.

– Albert Einstein

Montana is an ideal location for viewing wildlife in their natural habitat. Our state has more types of wildlife than any of the other lower 48 states. Many animals make their home in Montana's mountains and prairies and spotting them is truly spectacular.

Here are some wildlife viewing tips:

- Bring a map, guidebook or field guide for the area
- Try to think like an animal- familiarize yourself with their behaviors and habitat
- Most animals are most active at sunrise and sunset
- Watch for signs such as animal tracks or scat
- Carry binoculars
- Be very quiet and avoid wearing anything strongly scented
- Be patient

There are many designated wildlife viewing areas throughout the state. Check out Montana's tourism website for an excellent list of wildlife viewing areas as well as a list of wildlife guides and tours.

Here is one of my favorite wildlife viewing spots:

The National Bison Range

The National Bison Range might just be my favorite wildlife viewing location. It is located in the Mission Valley south of Flathead Lake in Moiese,

MT. It is a little off the beaten path, but it is truly a hidden gem. It was established in 1908 by President Roosevelt to conserve the bison species. Today there are between 250-300 bison in the herd.

For a very small fee, the refuge offers self-guided scenic drives, nature walks and fishing access. The refuge is open to visitors year round from dusk until dawn, but the visitor center has limited hours from October to May each year. Keep in mind that winter or hazardous weather may make the scenic roads impassible. Additionally, trailers of any kind, vehicles over 30 feet in length, motorcycles, ATVs and bicycles are not allowed on Red Sleep Mountain Drive.

When I visit the refuge, I like to start at the visitor center. There are some really neat and informative bison and wildlife displays to check out. They also have a map posted showing where wildlife has been seen that day. So take note of that and keep your eyes peeled in those areas especially. The range staff is always very helpful and love to share helpful viewing tips.

Next, head out for the scenic Red Sleep Mountain Drive. It takes about two hours, but plan to make plenty of stops along the way to view wildlife. You will undoubtedly see many bison and in the spring you may even see newly born bison. The refuge is also home to bear, pronghorn antelope, elk and many other animals.

On a recent trip in June, I was fortunate enough to see three black bears and one grizzly bear all from the safety of my car. My family and I watched two of the black bears turning over rocks on the hillside foraging for food for over an hour. We saw them running, playing with each other and even climbing trees. It was absolutely incredible and they were so close we didn't even need binoculars. One of the black bears walked so close to my car I could have reached out and petted it (Of course, I didn't!). We also saw bison, elk, deer, antelope and a bull snake.

After your scenic drive, stop by the picnic area and nature trail. I have seen some beautiful elk wandering through the picnic area. The nature trail is a short walk that loops around a small pond, which is usually full of turtles lying out on logs sunning themselves. I have even seen a couple gorgeous trumpeter swans.

31. WHAT YOU NEED TO KNOW ABOUT MONTANA'S WILDLIFE

The message is simple: love and conserve our wildlife.

– Steve Irwin

Montana is home to incredible wildlife. We have unique creatures, big and small. We also have many opportunities to enjoy exciting outdoor activities. This is awesome, but it often puts us right in Montana's wildlife habitats so there are a few things you should keep in mind when enjoying Montana's great outdoors.

Remember that Montana's wildlife deserve our respect. When we are in their habitat, we are in their home. It is important that we keep our disturbances minimal. This means leaving nature as we find it and packing out everything we pack in.

It also means giving the animals their space. It is awesome to see a bear or mountain goat, but remember this isn't a zoo. It is their home and we are the guests. Remember that you should never approach any kind of wildlife. Even the least intimidating animals can respond aggressively if they feel threatened. Besides, they have enough to worry about just trying to survive. They don't need us stressing them out.

We want you to have a positive experience in Montana. However, every year we have tourists that come into our state and act irresponsibly, giving tourists a bad name. Don't be that tourist taking selfies with a bison, feeding the bears or loading a baby wild animal into your car to *rescue* it. I wouldn't list these if they didn't actually happen. This type of behavior is dangerous for you, for the animal and it doesn't get you too many brownie points with the locals.

There are a couple of creatures, specifically, that you should be aware of in Montana because they can be dangerous to humans. Keep your eye out for rattlesnakes, ticks, mountain lions and bears. Here are a few tips on how to handle an encounter:

32. RATTLESNAKES

Ten snake species make their home in Montana, but only one species is venomous. The prairie rattlesnake, also known as the western rattlesnake, is a venomous pit viper. They can be shades of pale green to brown with darker brown or black blotches that are edged in a darker color. The blotches can turn to rings towards the tail. They have triangular-shaped heads, narrow necks and distinct rattles on their tail.

Luckily, rattlesnake bites in Montana are very rare (maybe a handful per year) and human deaths are even rarer (just about zero). Rattlers, as they are often called, prefer to avoid humans and will usually never bite unless they feel threatened. When you are in rattlesnake country, be aware of where you are walking or reaching and listen for the rattlesnake's warning rattle sound. If you encounter a rattlesnake, simply move away from the area and you should be fine.

In the very rare event that a rattlesnake does bite you or someone you are with, it is important to seek medical care immediately. Keep the person calm and their heart rate as low as possible. This can help slow the venom absorption. The area will begin to swell quickly so remove all jewelry or anything that may be constricting. Don't cut the wound, try to suck the venom out or apply a tourniquet. The most important thing is to get the snakebite victim to the hospital quickly. Trained hospital staff can administer antivenin, closely monitor the victim and treat any complications. Most people make a full recovery from rattlesnake bites when they are quickly treated.

33. TICKS

After a fun-filled day out under the big sky, the last thing you want to discover is that a tick has chosen to attach itself to you. Ticks are non-insect arthropod arachnids that may transmit several tick-born illnesses to humans. They are opportunistic creatures that crawl up on low plants and wait for animals to brush by them and then they attach to the animal to feed. In Montana, the Rocky Mountain wood tick is the most common and is most active from early spring to mid-July.

Wearing light colored clothing can help you to spot any ticks on your clothing. You can also tuck your pants into your socks to prevent them from crawling on your legs. Insect repellants are effective at deterring ticks. DEET insect repellants are very effective, but can be harmful for children. Check your body for ticks if you have been in an area where you might have encountered one.

Try not to panic if you do find a tick attached to you. The first thing you need to do is remove the tick. You should use tweezers or a notched tick extractor to grab the tick close to the skin and slowly and steadily pull up. Do not twist or jerk as you are pulling because this can cause the mouthparts to break off in the skin (Umm...Gross!).

After the tick is removed, thoroughly clean the bite area and any areas of the skin that may have come in contact with tick fluids. Place the tick in a sealed plastic bag or other container and save it in the freezer. If you become sick, your doctor may be able to use the tick to confirm whether or not you have a tick-born illness.

34. MOUNTAIN LIONS

Mountain lions, also known as cougars or pumas, are found throughout Montana. They are tawny in color and can reach up to seven feet in length from their nose to the tip of their tail and can weigh up to 180 pounds. They are territorial and usually claim a territory of 50 to 100 square miles or more.

They are strong predators that usually feed on deer, elk or smaller animals like mice or rabbits. They are capable of taking down a large animal several times their size. Like other cats, mountain lions stalk their prey and attack from behind, going for the head and neck. It is rare to spot a mountain lion in the wild. I have often heard that mountain lions will spot you before you spot them (creepy, right?).

Mountain lions often bury their kills so they can return to eat it later. If you happen to come across a dead animal that is hidden or partially buried, leave the area immediately. Mountain lions usually respond defensively when they feel their food source is being threatened.

If you happen to encounter a mountain lion while enjoying Montana's great outdoors, know that most mountain lions want to avoid you as much as you want to avoid them. You should face the lion at all times and do not bend over or crouch down. Pick up small children. The goal is to make yourself appear larger and threatening so you don't look like prey. You can raise your arms and make noise. Never run from a mountain lion or you could initiate an attack.

Mountain lion attacks in Montana are very rare (just about unheard of). If you are attacked, remember that many people have successfully fought off an attack by fighting back. Use whatever you have near you to fight off the lion. If you have bear spray, you can use that to deter the lion. It is also legal to use a firearm to defend yourself against a lion.

35. BEARS

Montana is home to both grizzly and black bears. We have more grizzly bears than any other state in the lower 48. Generally speaking, both grizzly and black bears prefer the mountainous western side of the state with black bears venturing farther east and all the way to the southeast corner of the state. Bears are spectacular animals and seeing one in the wild is truly a remarkable experience, but there are a few things you should know and precautions you should take.

First, don't feed the bears- intentionally or unintentionally. Food-conditioned bears, or bears that seek out human food, can be a nuisance or a danger to humans. It could also cost the bear its life. Many food-conditioned bears have to be euthanized in Montana each year because they become dangerous. So we all have a responsibility while in bear country to properly store our food and dispose of garbage in bear-proof receptacles.

Bears usually prefer to avoid humans and don't usually view us as prey. However, a bear can become defensive when you surprise them, when they think you are a threat to their food source or when you come between a mother bear and her cubs. Most bear encounters do not become conflicts and there are many things you can do to help prevent human-bear conflicts.

The best way to prevent a human-bear conflict is to avoid it altogether. When outdoors in bear country, let the bears know you are in their territory by making noise, singing or talking loudly. They will usually flee if they know you are there. Travel in groups and pay attention to your surroundings. Watch for signs of bears like tracks and bear scat. You should always carry bear spray and know how to use it (more on that later).

If you do encounter a bear, try to maintain a safe distance of at least 100 yards. Bears that don't immediately flee from you may exhibit defensive behavior. They might make a popping or clicking sound with their jaw or make snorting or huffing noises and paw at the ground. They might even lunge or charge towards you and stop (also known as a bluff charge). This is the bear telling you to leave.

You should respond by having your bear spray ready and talking calmly to the bear while slowly backing away. Don't make eye contact and try to be as non-threatening as possible. You could try throwing an object on the ground to distract the bear

123

if it is coming towards you, but you should keep your pack on your back to offer some protection in case you are attacked. If the bear continues towards you, you should deploy your bear spray. Once the bear stops or heads away from you, leave the area immediately.

Never run from a bear because this may trigger the bear to chase you and you won't be able to outrun it. Don't assume you are safe if you climb a tree either. Black bears are excellent tree climbers and grizzly bears are also very capable of climbing trees.

36. KNOW THE DIFFERENCE BETWEEN GRIZZLY AND BLACK BEARS

Black bears and grizzly bears are known to respond differently to humans so it is important to be able to identify each one. This can get a little confusing because black bears can be brown, cinnamon, blonde or a combination of colors. To make it even more confusing, grizzly bears aren't always, well, grizzled and their coats can also come in many color variations. Grizzly bears are generally larger than black bears, but that isn't a reliable identifying characteristic either. So what do you look for?

Look to their shoulders, facial profile, ears and claws. Grizzly bears are known for their distinguishable shoulder hump created by strong shoulder muscles. From the side, their shoulder hump will be higher than their rear end. Their facial profile is more concave with a wide prominent muzzle. Their eyes look close together and deeply set. They have small, rounded ears and long claws that are often light colored.

Black bears don't have a large shoulder hump like a grizzly bear. From the side view, their rear end or the middle of their back is higher than their shoulders. A black bear's facial profile is much straighter from their forehead to their nose. Their ears are larger and stick out farther from their head. They also have smaller claws that are more curved and are often darkly covered.

It can still be tricky to correctly identify a bear even knowing the identifying features of each one. I recommend visiting Get Bear Smart Society's website. They have detailed descriptions of grizzlies and black bears, excellent pictures and a fun bear identifying picture quiz. Hopefully you don't ever come close enough to a wild bear to inspect the size of its claws. However, if you do find yourself face to face with a bear, identifying the type of bear can help you determine how best to respond.

37. WHAT TO DO IF A GRIZZLY OR BLACK BEARS ATTACKS

You will know a bear is acting defensively if it is surprised by your presence or is defending its cubs or food source. It will likely exhibit the defensive behaviors discussed above. Most of the time a conflict can be avoided, but in case it is unavoidable you need to know what to do. Always have your pepper spray and be ready to use it.

Black Bear

If a black bear attacks you and pepper spray doesn't stop it, you may have to show them that you are standing your ground and are willing to fight back. If it comes to this, be ready to fight back aggressively with anything you can find and focus on hitting and kicking their face, eyes and snout. Usually, a black bear is not up for a big fight and will leave. DO NOT PLAY DEAD! Again, this is only for when a black bear defensively attacks.

Grizzly Bear

If a grizzly bear doesn't stop when sprayed with pepper spray and begins to attack you, the best thing to do is play dead. Lay on your stomach with your head and neck covered. Try not to let the bear roll you over. The grizzly will usually leave when they no longer view you as a threat. Stay in this position, not moving or making a noise, until you are sure the bear has left the area. You might have to stay like this for a very long time. However, if the bear continues attacking you or even eating you (OMG, right!) this isn't defensive grizzly behavior anymore and its time to defend yourself and try to fight back, going for the bear's face, eyes and nose.

Predatory Bears

An offensive bear is a predatory bear. When a grizzly or black bear offensively attacks, it is not acting to defend itself or its cubs or food. They will usually stalk their prey and attack from behind. They will not demonstrate any warning behaviors. They could also attack at night while you are sleeping in a tent. Although these encounters are extremely rare, it is important to know that your best chance of survival when attacked by a predatory bear is to fight back with everything you've got. DO NOT PLAY DEAD! The bear views you as prey in this situation and playing dead will literally give the bear a free meal.

38. WHAT YOU SHOULD KNOW ABOUT BEAR SPRAY

Bear spray is an aerosol containing capsicum. When sprayed at a bear, it temporarily inhibits the bear's ability to breath, see and smell. This usually delays the bear and allows you to get away. Do not use bear spray like you would insect repellent, applying it to your clothing or equipment. In fact, the smell could actually attract bears.

You can purchase bear spray in outdoor stores and many other stores located in bear country. Be sure it is EPA-approved bear spray and not any other personal defense spray. Counter Assault is a great brand and it is a made-in-Montana product. Bear spray has an expiration date so be sure yours isn't expired. Read the directions on your bear spray and know how to use it. You can purchase inert bear spray to practice if you would like. Counter Assault also makes inert bear spray.

Keep your bear spray where you can grab it quickly and not buried in a backpack. A holster on your hip works great. If you need to use it you will need to first remove the safety clip. You will want to spray slightly down and towards the bear when it is

30 to 60 feet away from you. The goal is to create a cloud of bear spray that the bear must pass through to get to you. Don't stop spraying until the bear heads away from you. If it doesn't stop, continue spraying the bear spray into the bear's face. Leave the area quickly after the bear has stopped charging you. Keep in mind that wind and weather can affect your spray.

At the end of your visit to Montana, hopefully you still have a full can of bear spray, but then you have to figure out what to do with it. It can't go on the plane home with you and it shouldn't be thrown directly in the trash. Donating it to another Montana adventurer before you leave is one idea. There are several places across Montana that recycle bear spray including hotels, visitor centers and ranger stations.

Many people choose to avoid the bear spray disposal issue altogether and rent their bear spray while they are here. This is a great option. It is much cheaper than purchasing a can of bear spray. Many bear spray rental companies also have trained staff on hand to give you advice and answer your questions. Most of the bear spray rental companies I have seen have been near Glacier and Yellowstone.

A Word About Bear Spray and Firearms

Most experts recommend bear spray to deter a bear over firearms. If you do have a firearm with you and know how to use it, it is legal in Montana to shoot a bear (or other animal) to defend yourself. However, not all guns are capable of taking a bear down. Keep in mind that shooting a bear, especially a grizzly bear, may not completely incapacitate it and a wounded bear may respond even more aggressively.

MORE UNIQUE MONTANA ADVENTURES

39. TAKE A HIKE...AND GET LOST

I took a walk in the woods and came out taller than the trees.

– Henry David Thoreau

While you are visiting Montana, you will undoubtedly see the popular green Montana shaped bumper stickers with the tagline *Get Lost (in Montana)*. The State of Montana Office of Tourism created this campaign to encourage people to get off the beaten path and really experience Montana. An excellent way to do just that is by taking a hike.

Montana is full of remarkable hiking adventures from short day hikes to weeklong backpacking trips. You can hike to gorgeous waterfalls, high mountain peaks or journey to sparkling alpine lakes. You can disconnect from the rest of the world and really get lost in Montana's wild beauty.

However, don't really get lost, lost. Things can turn ugly when that happens and you probably won't have cell service so you won't be able to call for help. So plan your route ahead of time and take a map and compass. Don't wander off of the trail. It is easy to get turned around when you aren't on the trail. Make sure others know where you plan to hike. Traveling with a group is a great idea too. Make sure you pack plenty of food, water and a first aid kit. Be sure to dress appropriately and be prepared for changing weather. Lastly, bring your bear spray and keep it handy.

The hardest part of hiking in Montana is deciding where you want to go. There are so many wonderful trails to choose from in all parts of the state. I have found a few resources have been helpful when planning hiking trips. Montana's tourism website has excellent Montana hiking resources and recommendations. The Montana Wilderness Association provides maps and detailed hike descriptions for many hikes across Montana. You will have a great time wherever you choose to hike, but here are two Montana hikes that I like:

One of my favorite Montana hikes is the Morrell Falls Trail north of the town of Seeley Lake. I like this hike because I really enjoy the gorgeous Morell

Falls at the end of the hike. The trail is right next to the Bob Marshall Wilderness and you will be in grizzly bear country so be bear aware. This trail is 5.4 miles round trip and is fairly easy. You will enjoy beautiful forests, two mountain lakes and the stunning 70-foot waterfall is well worth the hike.

Another unique hike is the Ice Caves Trail near Lewistown. This hike is rated intermediate to advanced and is about five miles in one direction. The views from the top of the Big Snowy Mountains are incredible and on clear days you can see for hundreds of miles. At some points the trail isn't visible, but follow the rock Cairns and you will reach Devil's Chute. This limestone cave holds snow and ice late into the summer. It has two main rooms connected by a tunnel if you are brave enough to explore it.

The Ice Cave is about a quarter mile past Devil's Chute. The floor of the cave is solid ice and the walls of the cave are marked by ice sheets and pillars. It is pretty neat to experience an ice cave, especially in the summer. After exploring the cave, you can return the way you came or make a loop and follow the Grandview Trail back.

40. ENJOY MONTANA'S INCREDIBLE LAKES, RIVERS AND WATERFALLS

*Eventually, all things merge into
one, and a river runs through it.*

– Norman Maclean

Montana is known for massive peaks, rolling prairies and the beautiful big sky. However, Montana is also home to an astonishing number of pristine lakes, rivers, streams and waterfalls. Montana has more than 3,000 named lakes and more than 150,000 miles of rivers, not to mention many incredible streams and waterfalls. Glacier National Park alone holds over 700 lakes, 563 streams and 200 waterfalls.

Montana's picturesque waters provide excellent fishing, fun water activities and incredible wildlife viewing opportunities. In the summer, the rivers and lakes are a welcome reprieve from the summer heat. Here are some of my favorite Montana water adventures:

Waterfall Adventures

Kootenai Falls off of Highway 2 between the towns of Libby and Troy is a site to behold. The Kootenai River drops an impressive thirty feet as it flows over the spectacular Kootenai Falls. This area is sacred to the Kootenai Indians, who use to live here and use this site to communicate with spiritual forces. The movies *River Wild* and *The Revenant* were also filmed here.

To get to the falls you will follow a trail through a forested area and across a covered pedestrian footbridge that crosses the railroad tracks. Then you will head down the trail to the Swinging Bridge. Crossing the bridge across the Kootenai River is a fun adventure. It isn't for everyone, but it is sturdy and gives the best view of the falls. You can also walk along the river to get a closer look at the falls.

You should know that although the trail isn't too strenuous, it can be rough and rocky in spots and you will also have to climb stairs to go over the footbridge. From May through September the parking lot has visitor information, souvenirs and food services. However, you can visit the falls in the winter too when the falls become a beautiful icefall.

Another amazing waterfall is Skalkaho Falls located along the Skalkaho Pass, which connects the

Flint Creek Valley to the Bitterroot Valley. The Salish Indian tribe traveled this pass long before it was a road and use to call it The Place of Many Trails. Today, the pass is only open seasonally. The road is located on the side of very steep mountains with no guardrails so it can be a little intense, especially when you are on the outer edge of the road when heading from the Bitterroot Valley to the Flint Creek Valley.

The drive to the falls is well worth the amazing view you will see just off the side of the road. The water plunges 150 feet down the falls and under the road. You can climb the side of the falls and sit along side of it as the water cascades past you. When I take this trip I usually like to make a day of it and stop in Philipsburg to visit the Sweet Palace and mine for sapphires at Gem Mountain Sapphire Mine.

Lake Adventures

There are many wonderful lakes to visit in Montana, but I am particularly partial to Flathead Lake. It is what remains of ancient Glacial Lake Missoula and is the largest freshwater lake west of the Mississippi. It is also one of the cleanest lakes in the world. You won't want to miss enjoying some delicious Flathead cherries while you are here and be sure to keep your eye out for the elusive Flathead Lake Monster. For over one hundred years people have reported seeing the mysterious monster, but nobody has been able to provide definitive proof.

Getting directly on the water with a boat, kayak or stand up paddleboard is my favorite way to explore the lake. There are several great rental businesses in the charming towns along the lake. Wild Horse Island State Park on the west shore is accessible only by boat and is an incredible place to visit and check out the scenery and wildlife. If you don't want to get on the lake, enjoying it from the shore is pretty spectacular too. There are several excellent public access sites around the lake that offer great swimming, picnicking and camping.

River Adventures

Montana's incredible rivers offer fun recreational activities ranging from swimming to fishing to boating and rafting. No matter where you are in the state, you won't have to travel far to reach one of our fantastic rivers. Here are some of my favorite river adventures:

Book a Rafting Trip

There are many excellent rafting guides throughout the state that offer rafting adventures for all ages and abilities ranging from calm water tours to high intensity whitewater rafting and overnight rafting trips. Montana's tourism website offers a great online tool to search for rafting guides in the area of Montana you plan to visit. Nothing beats the thrill of being on the river, feeling the water and passing through some of Montana's most picturesque scenery.

Float the River

One of Montana's favorite ways to beat the summer heat is to head out on the river on an inner tube (or canoe or kayak). Pack your cooler with refreshing drinks and spend the day basking in the sun as you float along the cool river. There are excellent floating rivers in every part of the state. Just don't forget your sunblock (I learned this the hard way one too many times). Be sure to pack out your trash and glass bottles are often not allowed on the river. Lastly, a life jacket is always a good idea just in case.

41. TRY YOUR HAND AT GOLD PROSPECTING AND ROCK HOUNDING

When it comes to rock hounding and gold prospecting, Montana lives up to its name as the Treasure State. Montana is known for its rich metal mining history. Which is why our state motto is *Oro y Plata*, Spanish for gold and silver. Montana also has two state gemstones: the Montana sapphire and Montana Agate. There are many places across the state where you can try your hand at gold prospecting and rock hounding. The search is always an exciting adventure, but taking home a sapphire, agate or other treasure that you found is the best souvenir. Here are a few great places:

Crystal Park

Located at 7,800 feet in the Pioneer Mountains near Dillon, Crystal Park is one of Montana's most popular rock hounding hotspots. Here you can search for quartz crystals across 220 acres. Bring your own digging tools and screens. Pack a lunch and make a day of it. The crystals aren't really worth anything, but they are beautiful and fun to find. I have never left Crystal Park without at least a dozen crystals. This is a great family activity and kids love it.

Gem Mountain Sapphire Mine

The Gem Mountain Sapphire Mine near Philipsburg is Montana's oldest sapphire mine. It is also one of largest sapphire deposits in the world. You can purchase Sapphire Gravel here and the trained staff will teach you how to wash it in the large outdoor troughs. Then you can take it to a table and pick through the gravel in search of your own sapphire treasures. When you are done take your sapphires inside and the staff will weigh and bag your sapphires for free. For a small additional fee, the trained staff will determine if your sapphires are gem quality. You can have your sapphire heat treated, faceted and even turned into jewelry or you can just take your beautiful stones home as is. I have never left empty handed when I've searched for sapphires at Gem Mountain Sapphire Mine. Since it is mostly located outdoors, the mine is only open seasonally. However, you can visit the Montana Sapphire Company's retail store in downtown Philipsburg year round. They sell beautiful sapphire jewelry and sapphires mined from Gem Mountain. You can even purchase sapphire gravel to take home or use the designated tables right in the store to search for sapphires.

Ruby Reservoir

The Ruby Reservoir is located off Montana Highway 287 near Alder. It has a primitive campground and restroom facility, but what makes this reservoir truly unique are the countless garnets lining the shoreline. You can walk along the shore and pick out flashes of red or dig through the dirt and search for the garnets. Some people have found success gold panning here as well. Visit during the fall when the water is lower and you might find more garnets.

River of Gold at Nevada City

Not too far from the Ruby Reservoir you can visit the River of Gold at the historic ghost town, Nevada

City. It is open from Memorial Day to Labor Day. This area has historically been rich in placer gold deposits. You can check out the ghost town, the mining equipment exhibits and learn how to gold pan. You might get lucky and find your own gold treasure. You can purchase an inexpensive package that includes a gold panning tutorial, the use of gold panning equipment and a vial to bring your gold and garnets home with you. It is fun for all ages.

Search for Moss Agates Along the Yellowstone River

The Yellowstone River in the eastern part of the state is one of the best places to find moss agates. These stones are semi-precious gemstone made from silicon dioxide. Minerals, often in shades of green, are present in the stone in different patterns giving the appearance of moss. Many people believe the agates have positive metaphysical properties. Historically, many Native Americans believed the moss agate was a stone of warriors and provided protection.

Finding one can require a lot of time and patience, but very little skill. You literally just have to walk along the river and look for moss agates. These beautiful agates can be kept as is or turned into beautiful jewelry.

143

42. FOLLOW THE DINOSAUR TRAIL

The Montana Dinosaur Trail is a trail spanning across the state that leads you to 14 different locations, each with unique opportunities to learn about the dinosaurs that once roamed Montana. If you have the chance to follow the trail, be sure to get your Montana Dinosaur Trail Passport. It is full of great information about each stop and if you receive all of the unique Dino Icon stamps within five years you will receive a reward. This is a fun activity for kids. It covers a lot of distance so it can be hard to visit all of it in one trip. However, visiting any one of the locations offers an incredible experience. Here are my favorites:

The Museum of the Rockies

The Museum of the Rockies is a must-see museum in Montana even if you don't plan to follow the dinosaur trial. It is a part of Montana State University and is affiliated with the Smithsonian. It is spectacular!

Big Mike, the bronze statue of MOR 555 (a T-Rex discovered in 1988 near Fort Peck Reservoir), will greet you from the front lawn as you arrive. Inside, you will enjoy viewing one of the largest collections of North American dinosaurs in the world (this is a pretty big deal!). On certain days, you can observe paleontologists preparing dinosaur fossils in the Bowman Dinosaur Viewing Laboratory. Besides the amazing dinosaur exhibits, the Museum of the Rockies is also known for its changing exhibits from around the world, the Martin Children's Discovery Center, the Taylor Planetarium and the Living History Farm, a life-size working 1890s Montana homestead. You won't want to miss the chance to visit this museum.

Makoshika State Park

Located southeast of Glendive, Makoshika State Park is Montana's largest state park. The name Makoshika means bad land in Lakota. The badlands offer stunning scenery to explore. The park is also known to be part of the late Cretaceous Hell Creek Formation. Many important dinosaur discoveries have been made here, including the discovery of more than ten different dinosaur species. Many of these discovery sites are marked for you to check out as you visit the park. The visitor center displays several great dinosaur fossils including a Triceratops skull.

As the weather continues to erode the land, more fossils are unearthed. Who knows, maybe you will find a fossil. However, digging is not allowed and neither is the removal of artifacts.

Two Medicine Dinosaur Center

The Two Medicine Dinosaur Center in Bynum is a unique stop along the trail because it offers regular people of all ages (children under 18 must be accompanied by an adult) the chance to participate in fossil searches, digs and the chance to help stabilize and extract fossils. The best time of the year to participate in these programs is in July and August. However, the digs fill up fast so you should contact the center up to a month before your trip to guarantee your spot. Also, you can't keep any of the fossils you find. They all have to be turned over to the center for research purposes, but nonetheless it is a great experience and you are helping to conduct real dinosaur research.

43. GET OFF THE BEATEN PATH— ATV EXPLORING AND 4X4 TRAILS

*Of all the paths you take in life,
make sure a few of them are dirt.*

– John Muir

Some of my greatest Montana memories have been made on 4-wheelers exploring remote parts of the state. I can remember spending entire days on a 4-wheeler following behind my grandpa Harold and great uncle Dale. They had spent their whole lives exploring and hunting in the mountains back behind town and enjoyed guiding us on family ATV trips. They led us to old abandoned mining camps, mountain lakes and through beautiful Montana scenery. They were the best guides, sharing historical stories and areas of geological significance. We would stop along the way to enjoy a delicious picnic lunch my grandma Flora and mom had packed. Those were the good old days!

You might not be able to hire my grandpa and great uncle as your guide. However, you can still

147

enjoy Montana's scenic 4x4 and ATV trails. There are many places across the state where you can rent an ATV and for some trails a truck or a jeep will get you there. You can also book a guided ATV tour through many ATV adventure companies as well as through many resorts.

If you want to venture off on your own, a local Montana couple, Willie and Jeanne Worthy have written several books with detailed descriptions of 4x4 routes in Montana. I have personally followed several of the routes in *4x4 Routes of Western Montana*. It really is the next best thing to actually having a tour guide with you. I have found the routes to be accurate with mile-by-mile directions and there are many points of interest listed along the way. They have led me to some amazing places including abandoned mines and beautiful alpine lakes.

A couple words of caution: Don't get lost. Montana's mountain roads and trails can be confusing. They often aren't marked well or even marked at all. It is easy to get turned around. Also, if you venture off very far you won't have cell service to call for help. So make sure you have a tour guide or a good map and let people know where you are going. It is a good idea to pack extra food, water, a first aid kit and extra clothing for changing weather.

44. MONTANA WINTER ADVENTURES

*For over 50 years I've traveled
the world with my skis and camera,
producing hundreds of ski movies.
One winter I was filming here in
Montana and I gave up traveling
forever. I could live anywhere in
the world, and I choose to live here
in Montana.*

– Warren Miller

In Montana, much of the state is buried under the snow for a good portion of the year. Fortunately, we don't all have to bunker down inside next to the fire for months on end. Although, that is a super cozy and perfectly acceptable way to spend the winter. No, adventures don't stop when the snow flies in Montana. In fact, for many people they are just getting started. Before heading out on any Montana winter adventure be sure you are prepared for the weather, dressed appropriately and understand and practice avalanche safety.

149

Here are a few of my favorite Montana winter adventures:

Skiing

In the winter, Western Montana becomes a ski and snowboarding paradise. Montana has about 15 ski resorts ranging in size from small resorts like my personal favorite, Discovery Ski Area, to one of the biggest ski resorts in North America, Big Sky Resort. There are plenty of excellent opportunities to get out and enjoy the fresh powder.

If sticking to the groomed trails isn't your style, there are several excellent locations for backcountry skiing. You can even hire a backcountry ski guide. Montana's tourism website is a great place to find out more about our ski resorts and backcountry ski guides.

Montana is also an excellent location to enjoy cross-country skiing. It isn't hard to find a good spot with Montana's many groomed cross-country trials. The town of Seeley Lake has been called *the best-kept Nordic secret in the Rockies* for its excellent groomed trails and ample snowfall.

Another version of skiing found in Montana is skijoring, which is basically skiing while being pulled behind a horse, sled dog or even a vehicle. In Montana you will likely find horse skijoring to be the most popular. You can try out skijoring at resorts like The Resort at Paws Up or Triple Creek Ranch. There are also several horse skijoring competitions you can watch in Montana. The Whitefish Skijoring World Invitational is a fun competition that is featured as part of Whitefish's famous Winter Carnival.

Snowshoeing

Many years ago snowshoes were a necessity for walking in deep winter snow. Today, snowshoeing is a fun winter activity. It doesn't require a whole lot of skill to snowshoe. People often say that if you can walk, you can snowshoe. There are many places to rent snowshoes throughout the state and it isn't hard to find a great snowshoe trail.

The Ross Creek Cedars Scenic Area near Troy is a great place to enjoy some snowshoeing. You can follow the 0.9-mile interpretive trail or continue on for another three miles to the cathedral-quiet grove. The snow on the giant cedars is a beautiful site (It's beautiful without snow too!).

Snowmobiling

Snowmobiling in Montana is an exciting, thrilling adventure. Montana is one of the best snowmobiling destinations in the country. We have thousands of miles of groomed and un-groomed trails to explore. Montana boasts just under 4,000 miles of groomed trails.

Many resorts such as the Three Bear Lodge in West Yellowstone and the Double Arrow Lodge in Seeley Lake become snowmobile resorts in the winter. You can also plan your own adventure and rent your equipment. Montana's tourism website is a great place to find snowmobile rentals locations. You can even find snowmobile guides for hire listed there. The Montana Snowmobile Association's website is a great place to learn more about where to snowmobile in Montana and how to stay safe.

Sledding

Sledding has always been a favorite winter pastime and for good reason. It is fun and inexpensive. All you need is snow, a sled and a good hill. You will find that many resorts will have sleds available for guests in the winter. You can also purchase them in most cities. Finding a good sledding hill isn't too difficult either. There are many across the state, too many to list here. A local would probably be happy to point you in the right direction to the nearest sledding hill.

Dog Sledding

If you visit Montana in the winter, a dog sledding adventure is a very unique experience. Imagine gliding across the snowy countryside on a sled pulled by a pack of dogs. You can do just that at many luxury resorts and several dog sled businesses across the state. Montana's tourism website has a good list of dog sled adventure companies. You can also attend a sled dog race. The Race to the Sky event usually occurs in February. You can watch the teams as they cross the finish line at Hi-Country Snack Foods in Lincoln.

Winter Sleigh Rides

A horse-drawn sleigh ride across a blanket of white snow is a great way to enjoy Montana's winter landscape. You can sit comfortably in the sleigh covered in warm blankets as your horses pull you through gorgeous snowy scenery. Many resorts offer this fun adventure as well as several winter sleigh ride businesses. Check out Montana's tourism website for a complete list.

45. ENJOY A RELAXING SOAK IN A MONTANA HOT SPRING

After an exciting day of adventuring in Montana, nothing tops the day off better than a relaxing soak in a hot spring. It is a great experience any time of year, but it becomes especially spectacular in the winter. You can relax in the warm water surrounded by snow as the steam rises above the water. Montana has many excellent hot springs worth visiting throughout the state. Montana's tourism website has a complete listing of Montana's hot springs as well as a map. Here are a few of my favorites:

Fairmont Hot Springs
Located just outside Butte, Fairmont Hot Springs holds one Olympic size indoor swimming pool and one large indoor hot pool. Outside you will also find another Olympic sized swimming pool and hot pool. There is also a 350 foot enclosed water slide that is open all year. I spent a lot of time here growing up and it is still one of my favorite Montana hot springs. You can stay at the resort or stop in just for a swim and soak. The naturally heated water is so relaxing. There is plenty to do nearby with an 18-hole golf

course on site, Discovery ski area nearby and the historic town of Butte just minutes away.

Quinn's Hot Springs Resort

Quinn's Hot Springs is located in Paradise (the town, although, you might feel like you are actually in paradise). Here, you can enjoy several outdoor geothermal heated chemical-free pools ranging in temperature from 89 degrees Fahrenheit to 106 degrees Fahrenheit. They also have an ice pool if you wish to give that a try. You can book a stay in their lodge or canyon, riverside or mountain cabins or drop in for a soak. They also have a great restaurant with locally sourced steak and a great wine list.

The Boiling River

The Boiling River is one of the few bits of Yellowstone National Park that Montanans get to proudly claim as our own. You will find this hot spring destination near the North Entrance to the park. The boiling river is part of the Gardiner River and gets its name from the hot spring water that runs into the river. The hot water mixes with the cool water of the river and creates a comfortable soaking experience. If you become too hot, just move further into the cooler water and vise versa. It is a pretty awesome experience! Where else can you soak in a boiling river on top of a supervolcano?

Stay directly out of the hot springs runoff channel though because you could be severely burned. The river is closed when the water is high in the spring. It also closes after dark. There is no skinny-dipping allowed and you can't bring alcohol into the river. Also, as the signs posted around the hot spring state, do not put your head under water or inhale the steam because the thermal water supports the growth of organisms that can cause serious health issues. Otherwise, it is safe to soak in.

46. LEARN ABOUT MONTANA'S MINING HISTORY IN BUTTE

At first look, you'd think this is the worst place on Earth. A ravaged, toxic, godforsaken hill threatened from above, riddled with darkness from below. But you'd be wrong.

– Anthony Bourdain

Butte is often underrated and overlooked as a fun tourist destination, but if you get the chance to visit Butte there is so much to see. Butte has one of the largest historic districts in the United States and there are plenty of opportunities to explore Butte's lively mining history.

Butte, hometown of daredevil Evil Knievel, was Montana's first major city and has been called *the richest hill on earth.* It began as a gold and silver mining camp in the 1860s and quickly became one of the world's biggest copper producers. At the end of the 19th century it was the largest city west of the Mississippi. There were once 74 mines in the area and

157

over 10,000 miles of underground tunnels. The Montana Bureau of Mines and Geology has mapped out the tunnels and those who are interested can purchase the map and see where the tunnels are located under present-day Butte.

Butte has a diverse population comprised of many ethnic groups. The area's rich mines attracted immigrants from all over the world including Ireland, Serbia and China. As of 2017, Butte was considered the most Irish places in the United States. Saint Patrick's Day is a big event in Butte and up to 100,000 people can show up to the parade. That is over triple Butte's normal population.

When you first arrive in Butte you will immediately notice the beautiful Lady of the Rockies looking down over the city from the continental divide. The Lady of the Rockies is a 90-foot statue built in the likeness of Mary, Mother of Jesus. Bob O'Bill completed the statue in 1985 with the help of many others. Mr. O'Bill built the statue after making a promise to build a statue if his wife survived cancer. He hadn't originally planned to make it so big, but the town came together and thought it would boost morale after the mines shut down. The statue is nondenominational and dedicated to women and mothers everywhere.

While you are in Butte, be sure to check out the many remarkable museums, mines and historical tours. The World Museum of Mining, which is located on an actual mine yard, is a great stop. Here you can explore the historic mining structures, fascinating exhibits and take a tour through a life-size accurately recreated 1860s mining town. Don't miss the underground mine tour, venturing 100 feet underground into the Orphan Girl Mine.

The Berkley Pit is also an interesting stop. You can look out over what was once a large open-pit copper mine. It has been filled with extremely toxic water for years. It is so toxic that it kills any birds that visit it. You can learn how the mining toxins have affected the community and what they are doing to remedy it. Just this year (2019) they have developed a system to clean the water from the pit and begin releasing it into nearby water sources.

The miners worked hard, but they played hard too. You can book an underground tour with Old Butte Historical Tours and see Butte's once thriving underground, which was built during the prohibition. The underground Rockwood Speakeasy is a highlight of the tour and has been preserved in almost perfect condition. Above ground, you can also check out the Dumas Brothel, which was one of the longest operating brothels in the United States, remaining open until 1982. It is also rumored to be haunted.

If you are up for some delicious Chinese food, be sure to visit the Pekin Noodle Parlor. This restaurant has been a local favorite since 1911. In fact, it is the oldest continuously operated Chinese restaurant in the United States. It might seem weird that the oldest Chinese restaurant is found in Butte, but you have to remember that during the mining boom immigrants came to Butte from all over the world. If you want to sample more of Butte's culinary flavors, be sure to sample a beef pasty or a pork chop sandwich, formerly known as the mining camp's version of fast food. Lydia's Supper Club is another great option and is Butte's only remaining Meaderville-style restaurant. Meaderville is Butte's Italian-American neighborhood. Lydia Micheletti began the restaurant many years ago and today it continues to be family ran and a local favorite.

47. BEST MONTANA GHOST TOWNS TO VISIT

The ghost towns of Montana offer a unique glimpse into Montana's history. In the late 1850s, gold was discovered in Montana and miners came to our state seeking wealth and prosperity. Thriving mining camps and eventually communities were erected near booming gold strikes. When the gold was gone, the people left, leaving behind entire towns. Today, many of these ghost towns are well preserved and you can walk through them, tour the buildings and imagine what life was once like in the booming mining towns. Here are a few great ghost towns to visit:

Garnet Ghost Town

My favorite ghost town to visit is Garnet Ghost Town. Located high in the Garnet Mountains, about forty miles east of Missoula, you can access Garnet from Highway 200 or Interstate 90. However, the road from I90 is rougher and not recommended for RVs or trailers. It is open year round, but in the winter it can be difficult to access.

At its prime, 1,000 people made their home in Garnet. There were many buildings including four stores, four hotels and even a school. The buildings constructed here were built quickly and without foundations. Many of the buildings were lost in a fire in 1912 and never rebuilt. Despite this, Garnet is one of Montana's most intact ghost towns.

Today you can take a tour (guided or self-guided) of the town's twenty or so buildings and learn more about the people that once called Garnet home. You can also check out the visitor center and gift shop. If you are feeling adventurous, you can take a short walk to the mysterious Coloma Ghost Town. It is a few miles north of Garnet and not much is known about it.

Bannack State Park

Bannack State Park near Dillon offers an incredible fifty or so structures to explore. People resided in Bannack from 1862 to the 1950s. Like most Montana ghost towns, it was a gold mining boomtown that was abandoned.

When you arrive, stop by the visitor center and grab a booklet to read about the history of each place as you walk along the tour. You can learn about Bannack's vigilante history and even try your hand at gold panning. Plan to spend at least a couple hours here. There is a lot to see.

Bannack Days is the third weekend in July and offers a great opportunity to celebrate the glory days of Bannack. You can enjoy breakfast in Hotel Meade, observe people demonstrating pioneer skills or ride through town in a horse drawn wagon. It is a really neat experience.

Virginia City and Nevada City

Virginia and Nevada City are located a short distance apart near the town of Ennis. Both towns offer a wonderful look into what is often called the richest gold strike in the Rocky Mountain West. You can take a scenic train ride between the two towns on the Virginia City Shortline. You can even stay in a historic hotel, cabin or vacation rental in both ghost towns.

Plan to spend at least a whole day here. These two towns offer a ghost town experience like nowhere else in Montana. There are so many things to see and do. Take a walking tour of both towns and imagine what it was like to live in a historic Montana mining town. Tour the Nevada City Living History Museum and Music Hall and learn what the mining towns were like during their prime. You can even try your hand at gold panning.

These two towns are serving up Montana history with a lively side of entertainment. Throughout the summer, you can come on the weekends for fascinating living history events. You can also watch the Virginia City Players Theatre Company perform melodramas and vaudeville acts in the Virginia City Opera House or enjoy a live comedy show with the Brewery Follies.

48. THE BRAWL OF THE WILD

The Brawl of the Wild is what Montanans call the annual November college football game featuring our state's rivaling teams, the Montana State Bobcats and the University of Montana Grizzlies. The game is also called the Cat-Griz game or Griz-Cat game. The rivalry began in 1897 and is still going strong today. In 2001, the Great Divide Trophy was created and each year the winning team gets the trophy and proudly displays it on their campus. The team that wins the most games between 2001 and 2099 will claim the trophy forever.

Montanans really get into this football game and the rivalry between Missoula's Grizzlies and Bozeman's Bobcats can be intense. Most Montana's are either diehard Griz or Cat fans, but not both (Go Griz!). If you are lucky enough to score tickets to The Brawl of the Wild, it is an awesome experience. Cities and towns across the state also broadcast the game in just about every bar and restaurant. You will find that watching the game with these fans is always an exciting event.

Montana has taken things a little further and for the past 20 years we hold a friendly food drive competition between Missoula and Bozeman. The town with the most food collected wins. Every year the food drive is a great success and fills the Missoula Food Bank and the Gallatin Valley Food Bank with cash donations and thousands of pounds of food. If you are visiting Montana during the Month of November keep your eye out for collection sites and fill free to help support a great cause.

49. UNIQUE MONTANA FESTIVALS TO CHECK OUT

Montana offers many great music festivals throughout the state including the Red Ants Pants Music Festival in White Sulphur Springs, Rockin' The Rivers in Three Forks, Headwaters Country Jam in Three Forks and Magic City Blues in Billings. Most music festivals occur during the warmer summer months.

Here are some other unique Montana festivals to check out:

The Montana Folk Festival occurs each July in Butte's historic district. It is free to all and offers excellent music, delicious food and drink and the chance to check out Montana's local artists. This festival holds the Montana Traditions Art Market featuring local artists and the First Peoples' Market featuring Native American artists and craftspeople.

Brothel Days in Virginia City is a unique festival in June that pays tribute to the workingwomen that were an important part of the mining boomtown's history. These women worked as prostitutes and hurdy-gurdy girls, or ladies that served drinks and danced with the miners. At the festival you can take in historical presentations, participate in or watch the bed races down the street, enjoy good music and even dress up for a brothel-themed costume dance party.

For more than 40 years, the August Huckleberry Festival in Trout Creek has been the place to go to celebrate Montana's delicious purple berry. You can enjoy a huckleberry pancake breakfast, try every type of huckleberry food you can imagine, check out the work of local artists and even participate in a huckleberry-baking contest. There is also a parade, talent contest, horseshoe contest and 5k Run for Fun.

The An Ri Ra Montana Irish Festival in August in Butte's original mine yard is one of the greatest Irish Festivals in North America. Here you can celebrate Irish heritage by participating in educational events, attending Irish mass, listening to Montana and Irish authors and enjoying great music and Irish dancing. The admission is free and all ages are welcome.

The River City Roots Festival in Missoula is a two-day festival in August in downtown Missoula. You can enjoy a fine art show, a 4-mile fun run and excellent live music. For children, the Family Fun Fest is a great place to enjoy fun activities and children's music. It is fun for the whole family and admission is free.

In the winter, the Whitefish Winter Carnival has been the place to be for over fifty years. Here you can, learn about the Nordic winter god, Ullr and participate in fun winter activities. You can support the Special Olympics by participating in the Penguin Plunge and jumping into the icy Whitefish Lake. You can also enjoy the Grand Parade and watch the skijoring competition.

50. SOUVENIRS TO BRING HOME

Travel changes you. As you move through this life and this world you change things slightly, you leave marks behind, however small. And in return, life – and travel – leaves marks on you. Most of the time, those marks – on your body or your heart – are beautiful.

– Anthony Bourdain

Unfortunately, you can't bring Montana home with you. However, you can bring mementos to remind you of your wonderful visit. Photographs are my absolute favorite souvenirs. They are free to take and thank goodness for that because I love to take pictures of everything when I visit a new place. I enjoy sharing my experiences with family and friends and photos are an excellent way to do that. Plus, every time I look at my photos I am taken back to that moment perfectly preserved in a photo.

Beyond the basic souvenir ideas, here are a few unique Montana souvenir ideas:

- Montana Huckleberry products- jam, syrup, chocolate, saltwater taffy- you name it! Or better yet, bring the fresh huckleberries you picked home!
- Flathead Lake cherries
- Handcrafted Montana chocolate or candy
- Montana made honey
- Montana made jerky
- Montana roasted coffee or tea
- Montana made craft beer, distilled spirits or wine
- Montana's Special Spice- Alpine Touch Seasoning
- Made in Montana art, jewelry or pottery
- Native American Made in Montana American Indian artwork
- Montana apparel from Montana Shirt Co.
- Montana rocks and sapphires that you found (from an approved location)

TOP REASONS TO BOOK THIS TRIP

The Gorgeous Scenery-

Montana holds some of the most beautiful scenic views in the country! Snow-capped mountain peaks, sparkling glacier fed waters, meadows filled with wildflowers, sweeping plains, stunning badlands and the biggest sky you've ever seen - this is Montana! You will find impressive beauty in every corner of our state.

The Incredible Wildlife-

Much of Montana is wild and untouched, allowing the wildlife to roam free in their natural habitat. Montana's varied landscape gives rise to an abundance of diverse wild animals. You won't have to look very hard to spot spectacular wild animals including bear, moose and elk.

Vast Open Space-

You won't feel overcrowded here. Montana is a welcome escape from the busy urban lifestyle! As one of the least populated states, Montana offers ample open space to explore and the peace and quiet

171

you crave. Not to mention, all the fresh air you can breathe.

Exciting Outdoor Adventures-

Montana is an outdoor adventure destination! Whether you want to hike to a remote glacier, whitewater raft down an exhilarating river or try your hand at fly-fishing, Montana has you covered. Every season brings new adventures!

Food-

Montana is a culinary treasure trove of delicious food often made from locally sourced ingredients. You will find roadside stands and farmer's markets selling locally grown produce, charming mom and pop restaurants plating up tasty home-style meals and fine dining restaurants serving delectable dishes made from local ingredients. From our native huckleberries to our grass-fed beef, you will be sure to find something to satisfy your taste buds.

People-

Montana's unique vibe and friendly people are part of what makes Montana the *Last Best Place*. Our diverse mix of people includes cowboys and ranchers, Native Americas, artists and writers and hard-working folks. You will love Montana's culture, welcoming hospitality and country charm!

OTHER RESOURCES

All of these websites were a great help to me while writing this book. Each one is worth checking out for further information.

Montana Official State Website
https://www.mt.gov

Montana Tourism
https://www.visitmt.com

Montana Fish, Wildlife and Parks
https://fwp.mt.gov

Montana Historical Society
https://mhs.mt.gov

Montana Kids
https://montanakids.com

Montana Maps
https://mdt.mt.gov/publications/maps.shtml

Montana State Parks
https://stateparks.mt.gov

Glacier and Yellowstone Parks

https://nps.gov

Distinctly Montana

https://distinctlymontana.com

Made in Montana and Native American Made in
Montana

https://madeinmontanausa.com

Get Bear Smart Society

https://bearsmart.com

Forest Fire Prevention

https://www.keepgreen.org/home.html

PACKING AND PLANNING TIPS

A Week before Leaving

- Arrange for someone to take care of pets and water plants.

- Email and Print important Documents.

- Get Visa and vaccines if needed.

- Check for travel warnings.

- Stop mail and newspaper.

- Notify Credit Card companies where you are going.

- Passports and photo identification is up to date.

- Pay bills.

- Copy important items and download travel Apps.

- Start collecting small bills for tips.

- Have post office hold mail while you are away.

- Check weather for the week.

- Car inspected, oil is changed, and tires have the correct pressure.

- Check airline luggage restrictions.

- Download Apps needed for your trip.

Right Before Leaving

- Contact bank and credit cards to tell them your location.

- Clean out refrigerator.

- Empty garbage cans.

- Lock windows.

- Make sure you have the proper identification with you.

- Bring cash for tips.

- Remember travel documents.

- Lock door behind you.

- Remember wallet.

- Unplug items in house and pack chargers.

- Change your thermostat settings.

- Charge electronics, and prepare camera memory cards.

READ OTHER
GREATER THAN A TOURIST
BOOKS

179

> TOURIST

Follow us on Instagram for beautiful travel images:

http://Instagram.com/GreaterThanATourist

Follow *Greater Than a Tourist* on Amazon.

>Tourist Podcast

>T Website

>T Youtube

>T Facebook

>T TikTok

>T Goodreads

>T Amazon

>T Mailing List

>T Pinterest

>T Instagram

>T Twitter

>T SoundCloud

>T LinkedIn

>T Map

> TOURIST

At *Greater Than a Tourist*, we love to share travel tips with you. How did we do? What guidance do you have for how we can give you better advice for your next trip? Please send your feedback to GreaterThanaTourist@gmail.com as we continue to improve the series. We appreciate your constructive feedback. Thank you.

METRIC CONVERSIONS

TEMPERATURE

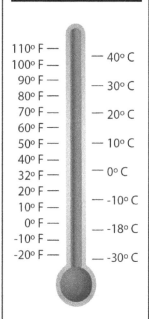

110° F —
100° F —   — 40° C
90° F —
80° F —   — 30° C
70° F —   — 20° C
60° F —
50° F —   — 10° C
40° F —
32° F —   — 0° C
20° F —
10° F —   — -10° C
0° F —   — -18° C
-10° F —
-20° F —   — -30° C

To convert F to C:

Subtract 32, and then multiply by 5/9 or .5555.

To Convert C to F:

Multiply by 1.8 and then add 32.

32F = 0C

LIQUID VOLUME

To Convert:................Multiply by
U.S. Gallons to Liters............... 3.8
U.S. Liters to Gallons 26
Imperial Gallons to U.S. Gallons 1.2
Imperial Gallons to Liters....... 4.55
Liters to Imperial Gallons 22
1 Liter = .26 U.S. Gallon
1 U.S. Gallon = 3.8 Liters

DISTANCE

To convert ....Multiply by
Inches to Centimeters 2.54
Centimeters to Inches 39
Feet to Meters...................... .3
Meters to Feet 3.28
Yards to Meters 91
Meters to Yards 1.09
Miles to Kilometers 1.61
Kilometers to Miles............ .62
1 Mile = 1.6 km
1 km = .62 Miles

WEIGHT

1 Ounce = .28 Grams
1 Pound = .4555 Kilograms
1 Gram = .04 Ounce
1 Kilogram = 2.2 Pounds

TRAVEL QUESTIONS

- Do you bring presents home to family or friends after a vacation?

- Do you get motion sick?

- Do you have a favorite billboard?

- Do you know what to do if there is a flat tire?

- Do you like a sun roof open?

- Do you like to eat in the car?

- Do you like to wear sun glasses in the car?

- Do you like toppings on your ice cream?

- Do you use public bathrooms?

- Did you bring a cell phone and does it have power?

- Do you have a form of identification with you?

- Have you ever been pulled over by a cop?

- Have you ever given money to a stranger on a road trip?

- Have you ever taken a road trip with animals?

- Have you ever gone on a vacation alone?

- Have you ever run out of gas?

- If you could move to any place in the world, where would it be?

- If you could travel anywhere in the world, where would you travel?

- If you could travel in any vehicle, which one would it be?

- If you had three things to wish for from a magic genie, what would they be?

- If you have a driver's license, how many times did it take you to pass the test?

- What are you the most afraid of on vacation?

- What do you want to get away from the most when you are on vacation?

- What foods smell bad to you?

- What item do you bring on ever trip with you away from home?

- What makes you sleepy?

- What song would you love to hear on the radio when you're cruising on the highway?

- What travel job would you want the least?

- What will you miss most while you are away from home?

- What is something you always wanted to try?

- What is the best road side attraction that you ever saw?

- What is the farthest distance you ever biked?

- What is the farthest distance you ever walked?

- What is the weirdest thing you needed to buy while on vacation?

- What is your favorite candy?

- What is your favorite color car?

- What is your favorite family vacation?

- What is your favorite food?

- What is your favorite gas station drink or food?

- What is your favorite license plate design?

- What is your favorite restaurant?

- What is your favorite smell?

- What is your favorite song?

- What is your favorite sound that nature makes?

- What is your favorite thing to bring home from a vacation?

- What is your favorite vacation with friends?

- What is your favorite way to relax?

- Where is the farthest place you ever traveled in a car?

- Where is the farthest place you ever went North, South, East and West?

- Where is your favorite place in the world?

- Who is your favorite singer?

- Who taught you how to drive?

- Who will you miss the most while you are away?

- Who if the first person you will contact when you get to your destination?

- Who brought you on your first vacation?

- Who likes to travel the most in your life?

- Would you rather be hot or cold?

- Would you rather drive above, below, or at the speed limited?

- Would you rather drive on a highway or a back road?

- Would you rather go on a train or a boat?

- Would you rather go to the beach or the woods?

TRAVEL BUCKET LIST

1.

2.

3.

4.

5.

6.

7.

8.

9.

10.

NOTES

CPSIA information can be obtained
at www.ICGtesting.com
Printed in the USA
LVHW031031221119
638065LV00006B/2293/P